D1164094

AMERICAN EDUCATION

Its Men

Ideas

and

Institutions

Advisory Editor

Lawrence A. Cremin
Frederick A. P. Barnard Professor of Education
Teachers College, Columbia University

LA
212
R52

Scientific Management in Education

J. M. Rice

ARNO PRESS & THE NEW YORK TIMES
*New York * 1969*

C49477

THE LIBRARY
INDIANA STATE UNIVERSITY
EVANSVILLE CAMPUS

WITHDRAWN

Reprint edition 1969 by Arno Press, Inc.

*

Library of Congress Catalog Card No. 70-89225

*

Manufactured in the United States of America

Scientific Management in Education

SCIENTIFIC MANAGEMENT IN EDUCATION

BY DR. J. M. RICE

Author of

"THE PUBLIC SCHOOL SYSTEM OF THE UNITED STATES,"
"THE RATIONAL SPELLING BOOK," ETC.

HINDS, NOBLE & ELDREDGE
NEW YORK PHILADELPHIA
1914

Copyright, 1912, by
J. M. RICE

INTRODUCTION

This book consists of a collection of twelve articles bearing upon the causes of success and failure in the teaching of the so-called essential branches in the elementary schools. The essays, which were based on tests extended to a large number of children attending schools in various parts of our country, were published at intervals in *The Forum*. Although the total number of pupils examined was not far from 100,000, I did not utilize the work of more than some 50,000 for strictly scientific purposes. Upon the other papers, I did considerable labor as well, but I decided to discard them because the investigation was interrupted for a time through pressure of work after I had become the editor of the magazine, and I thought it advisable to begin anew with fresh material when its conversion into a quarterly gave me the required leisure to resume it. Moreover, I also felt that I could safely dispense with the older papers, as I was satisfied before publishing the later articles that the 50,000 sufficed to furnish all the data needed to answer the purpose for which the tests had been intended.

The material that I shall place before the reader will be presented in practically the same form in which the articles originally appeared. By means of a careful revision, it would have been possible for me to curtail the discussion to some extent in the first four chapters. However, as, in certain respects, the work is admittedly the first of its kind that has ever appeared in print,[1] I decided, if only for whatever historical interest there may be in it, to give it here substantially as it first appeared. Moreover, with a single exception, the articles are in their original order. The exception was made in the case of the chapter on Educational Research, to which, by reason of its scope, I gave the leading position, although, chronologically, it would be the sixth.

The motive that had prompted me to take upon my shoulders this task—which, as the reader may well imagine, was not a very simple one—was the desire to learn whether or not it was possible so to extend the curriculum as to include the subjects demanded by the new school of education without detriment to the three R's. In the series of articles that I had previously written for *The Forum* as a result of visits to the schools of thirty-six cities,[2] I had laid stress not so much on results as on the contrast in the class-room spirit that existed between the old-fashioned, mechanical schools, with their narrow curriculum, on the one hand, and the

[1] See Note at close of Introduction.

[2] The series was composed of nine articles which appeared in the issues from October, 1892, to June, 1893, inclusively. The essays, with considerable additional material, were subsequently published in book form by the Century Company, as "The Public School System of the United States."

modernized schools, with their extended curriculum, on the other. And while few, if any, appeared to express doubt in regard to the desirability of maintaining the modern spirit, doubt was expressed on many sides from the standpoint of practicability, the claim of the doubters being that, when too many branches were introduced, and things were made too pleasant for the children, the results in the essentials were bound to suffer. In opposition to this, however, the progressives claimed that the new spirit and curriculum did not tend in the least to militate against results in the essentials, but that, on the contrary, the pupils in their schools were much better grounded in the essentials than those in the old-fashioned, mechanical schools, with their much narrower curriculum.

As the question here involved was clearly one of facts, I at least attempted to settle the controversy from that standpoint, thus making a departure from the course ordinarily pursued in endeavoring to solve problems in the educational field. Nor do I believe that the attempt was made altogether in vain, because I feel confident that I have discovered not only the fundamental cause of the unsatisfactory results that are found in so many of the elementary schools of our country, but also a remedy that is capable of eliminating it. Moreover, the remedy does not partake of the nature of a fad, but is also fundamental in character, because it means no less than the introduction of scientific management into the conduct of our schools.

In speaking of scientific management, in this connection, the reader will be likely to gain the impression that I am referring to the business side of school affairs, while, in fact, it is the educational side that I have in mind. The school has but a single purpose, which is that of educating children. Consequently, in the strict sense, scientific management in education can only be defined as a system of management specifically directed toward the elimination of waste in teaching, so that the children attending the schools may be duly rewarded for the expenditure of their time and effort. And, as will be seen in the text, my investigation indicated that, insofar as the results in the essentials were concerned, this was the case in not over one-third of the schools examined, two-thirds of them falling below a reasonable minimum standard, and half of these very far below, the difference between the best and the poorest third representing the equivalent of about two years of schooling, while in the more extreme instances the difference was even greater. But these figures do not show the whole truth, because this is not appreciated until we consider the other side of the story, namely, that when the pupils of the poorer schools graduate after an attendance of eight years, they are no farther advanced than the pupils of the better schools who are still in the fifth or sixth grade, and therefore have from two to three years of elementary education still before them.

That a phenomenon of this nature would appear to indicate that there was something wrong with the management in education goes without saying.

There is, indeed, but one contingency that would serve to render such a conclusion invalid, namely, that the differences in the results could have been accounted for by the differences in the conditions. However, as I was fully aware, before starting the investigation, that the results of my tests would be worthless for scientific purposes unless the conditions were fully considered, I made an effort to study the latter from every conceivable point of view, so that, in this regard, my work is not vulnerable. Indeed, I carried the idea so far that the working tables upon which my articles on spelling were based contained no less than sixty-eight columns, one of these only showing the results, while sixty-seven showed the conditions. This matter will be fully commented on in the respective chapters; but I wish to say here in passing that the differences in the results could not be accounted for by the difference in the conditions, excepting, perhaps, to a very small extent. For this reason, but one deduction from my tests is possible, namely, that the differences in the results were due to differences in the quality of the teaching, so that it is upon this side that we must concentrate our attention in our efforts to improve the schools.

That the business affairs of the schools should also be managed scientifically goes without saying, because there is naturally an advantage in an administrative system that works smoothly and efficiently, and without unnecessary waste of funds. But matters that strictly belong to the functions of the school board bear no direct logical relation to the results obtained in the individual branches in the class-room; the latter being a field that lies altogether within the province of the professional corps. The school board, as a body representing the people, may be logically empowered to determine what branches shall be taught beyond the essentials, and also to decide what shall be done for the benefit of the exceptional children, as well as what special institutions shall be maintained. Or, in other words, it has a logical right to attend to all matters that could be intelligently determined by the referendum. This, moreover, would include the power to make at least certain appointments to the educational staff, although how far it should be empowered to go in this direction beyond the appointment of the superintendent is still regarded as a debatable question.

If it should be given the authority to go very far, it is evident that it could exert an unfavorable influence on the results, in the positive sense, by failing to make the best appointments for the money at its disposal, thereby affording an opportunity for the educational heads to shift the responsibility for the results, at least in part, upon the shoulders of the members of the school board. And what is true of the appointment of the educational workers is no less true of their discharge. However, assuming that the conditions are such in any given locality that the members of the board are actuated by the highest motives only, and therefore make it possible for the educators to travel along the lines of least resistance in developing the educational work—a condition that is not infrequently found—the board does not thereby exert a favorable influence on the results, in the positive sense. What it does, under those circumstances, means no more than to refrain from putting any needless obstructions in the way of the educators, as a consequence of which the responsibility for the results in the branches that are taught is placed where it properly belongs, namely, upon the educational heads.

The philosophy of this is that, while a board composed of members who are disposed to take advantage of their powers for selfish ends, whether political or otherwise, may directly exert an unfavorable influence on the results, this cannot be said of the converse, because the highest stand that a board can take in respect to the attainment of results, insofar as the curriculum extends, is the negative one of refraining from hampering the educational workers in their efforts to obtain the best possible results. And the negative stand cannot, of course, exert any direct influence on the side of improvement, because results do not spring into being spontaneously.

The ideal basis for the achievement of results, then, would appear to be represented by a system under which the educational heads were given full opportunity to do what they believed to be the best in regard to the branches that they were authorized to teach, among which, naturally, the three R's are always included. Now, what we should expect to find, under these circumstances, would be, of course, that the results were on a higher plane in the localities where the schools were conducted on that basis than in those where they were not. As it so happens, however, that the data collected during my investigations failed to show any such condition, it is evident that the mere separation of the business from the educational side of school affairs will not in itself suffice to assure the achievement of satisfactory results. That the separation would serve to pave the way for the attainment of the best possible results in the class-room seems to me to be non-debatable. But my data would appear to prove that actual success cannot be depended upon even under those conditions unless the proper thing is done by the educational workers after they have been given their pedagogical freedom.

That, from the standpoint of scientific management, the school board cannot be regarded as the head of the educational department in matters pedagogical may be made clear in a very few words. Thus, the pedagogical system, as a unit, may be looked upon as a series of five elements placed one above the other; being, from below upward, the child, the teacher, the principal, the superintendent, and the top. In practice, things are so arranged that the child is instructed and supervised by the teacher, the teacher by the principal, and the principal in turn by the superintendent. This arrangement is theoretically justified on the ground that, in the pedagogical sense, the teacher is supposed to be wiser than the child, the principal than the teacher, and the superintendent than the principal. Leaving aside the fact that this theory does not always hold in practice—because not all principals are pedagogically wiser than their teachers or all superintendents than their principals—and assuming that it does, then it is obvious that we can only go from the sublime to the ridiculous if we place above the superintendent, for the purpose of directing him pedagogically, persons who are not supposed to have any pedagogical qualifications whatever; so that, from this point of view, they can only be looked upon, theoretically, as occupying a position that is even a step lower than that of the teacher, being, in fact, intermediate between herself and the child.

Now, when, in consequence of the recognition of the contradiction, the educational is separated from the business department, this particular absurdity is eliminated. Nevertheless, that a change of this nature does not constitute a solution of the problem is evident from the fact that it simply takes away the restraining hand of the board, without putting anything else in its place. In other words, what happens, under those circumstances, is that a transformation takes place as a result of which there is no longer in existence an authorized entity that stands above the superintendent, to whom he is directly responsible for his work. In this way, the superintendent becomes the official top of the system—a law unto himself, and the sole judge of his own efficiency. Under these conditions, the results achieved in the schools of his community will be purely a matter of chance. If he has the qualifications needed to bring about efficiency, the general run of the work in his schools will be good; if not, it will be poor; and the children must be satisfied with what they get.

In my opinion, then, the solution of the problem will lie not in eliminating the fifth element, thus converting the superintendent into the top, but in placing at the top, in lieu of the school board, an entity to which the superintendent will be logically subordinate in the pedagogical sense, however great his qualifications may be, or however great they may become. This means that we must use as the top something that will be intrinsically worthy of recognition as such at all times and under all conditions, and above which no logical one is either possible or conceivable. This is neither more nor less than the truth, to the extent that it is known. In practice, this would be represented objectively by a series of standards based upon the results that have been achieved in the more successful schools laboring under ordinary conditions.

While standards of this nature do not yet exist, the facts to be presented in this book will suffice to prove that their establishment lies well within the range of possibility. And when they shall have been not only established, but utilized in the proper way, there is no reason why the schools should not be, on the whole, very much improved. Although a system of this nature could not be expected to bring about perfection, there is no doubt that it could at least serve to lead to a very much greater degree of equality than we have to-day, and this mainly as a result of raising the standard of the truly weak schools to such an extent that they would be able to meet the requirements of a fixed reasonable minimum.

A scientific system of pedagogical management would demand fundamentally the measurement of results in the light of fixed standards. But while this proposition will no doubt seem both reasonable and plausible to the uninitiated, it nevertheless stands for a complete revolution in the educational field, because under its terms the basis of supervision would be no longer represented by personal opinions, but by standards based on facts derived from the school of universal experience. And if we wish to accept this as a guide in the conduct of our schools, it will simply be necessary to inaugurate a system with that in view. In the individual chapters, we shall feel our way toward the goal; and in the final one I have given the outline of a plan that I look upon, at least in the main, as both practical and feasible.

What must, of course, be borne in mind is that the establishment of standards will not in itself suffice to raise the results to a higher plane, as it is evident that this can do no more than furnish us with a rational basis for laboring in the right direction. In order that the standards might serve the purpose for which they were intended, it would be necessary to see that they were properly utilized by the superintendent. This, however, could not be depended upon unless some form of supervision should be exercised over the superintendent himself. At the first glance it might appear that this suggestion simply carried us back to our starting point in calling for a human element to direct the work of the superintendent. But this is a mere delusion, because the supervision would be exercised from an entirely different standpoint. Thus, what would now be done would not lie in telling him what to do and how to do it, but the supervision over him would be limited to a study of the results achieved in the individual schools and class-rooms, and then seeing that the work was improved in those instances in which it did not come up to the demanded standard. And, if the standards should be clearly defined, this would not require any special pedagogical insight, but would be a matter coming within the range of any intelligent citizen sufficiently interested in learning whether the school attended by his own children was doing as well as it could be expected to do under the existing conditions.

In conclusion, I desire to say a word in regard to what I look upon as the essential difference between scientific and unscientific management. And I cannot express my views upon this subject more tersely than to declare that, in my opinion, the former bears the same relation to the latter as the conception of universal bears to that of individual experience. Thus, as I see it, scientific management indicates that it is the intention of the department to direct its activities upon the basis of the best that is known, and unscientific management the intention to direct them upon the basis of the past experiences of the individual at the top, regardless of what those of others may have been in regard to the issues in question. Consequently, under unscientific management, the one at the top is a law unto himself, while, under scientific management, he is subordinate to the higher law. Or, in other words, in the one case the individual occupies a position above the universal, while in the other he occupies a position subordinate to it. And no extended discussion is required to explain how inordinately wasteful the methods are liable to become when the person in charge fails to avail himself of the benefit of the knowledge to be derived as a result of the combined experiences of the hosts of others who have labored in the same field.

Since the publication of the last article in this series, I have given a great deal of thought to the particular nature of the force that would be required to prevent the individual at the top from taking a position above the truth, that is, a position where he would have an opportunity to ignore the facts derived from universal experience, and, instead, give to his own opinions the right of way. And, as a result of such reflection, I have succeeded in devising a method of supervision on a basis that would, I believe, make it possible for us to carry out this ideal in practice. Naturally, a plan of supervision of this nature would not apply to education alone, but would be applicable to all departments in the public service. The work in which the idea is embodied will logically follow the present one.

Note.—In support of my statement that this is admittedly the first work of the kind to appear in print, I shall quote a few references. The passages are particularly gratifying to me because of the rather unusual circumstance that the results of the initial investigation were so very closely, if not completely, verified by those that were subsequently made by others.

"Educational Psychology," by Edward L. Thorndike, Professor of Educational Psychology, Teachers' College, Columbia University:

"Dr. Rice's study is quoted at some length, because it was the first of a series of studies of the actual results of school work, still few in number, but destined to increase rapidly with increasing scientific interest in school administration." (Pp. 125 and 126.)

"The near future will doubtless see a rapid increase in the number and improvement in the quality of studies of the environmental causes of individual differences in mental traits. Rice's investigation of the differences due to different features of administration and teaching has been followed by similar studies by Cornman ('02), Stone ('08), Courtis ('09), and Thorndike ('10). Experts in education are becoming experimentalists and quantitative thinkers, and are seeking to verify or refute the established beliefs concerning the effects of educational forces upon human nature. Students of history, government, sociology, economics, ethics, and religion are becoming, or will soon become, quantitative thinkers concerning the shares of the various physical and social forces in making individual men differ in politics, crime, wealth, service, idealism, or whatever trait concerns man's welfare." (P. 135.)

"Spelling in the Elementary School," by Dr. Oliver P. Cornman, Asst. Supt. of Schools, Philadelphia, Pa.:

"One extensive statistical inquiry, however, has been conducted by Dr. J. M. Rice. Conspicuous not only for the singularity of its presence within the field of pedagogical discussion, but equally so for the skill and discernment with which it was carried to a conclusion, this investigation has done much to clear up vague opinions as to the place of spelling in the elementary school, and to establish many important facts concerning the effect of the age, environment, etc., of the pupil, and of the methods and other factors of teaching upon the results of instruction. The writer has found this investigation very suggestive, and has employed some of Dr. Rice's tests in experiments to be described later." (P. 5.)

"I have quoted this conclusion of Dr. Rice's because it paraphrases so well the deductions which I believe should be made from the evidence which has been submitted, and it seems especially appropriate to emphasize in this way the arrival at the same point by two such different routes as those taken by Dr. Rice and the writer." (P. 39.)

"These conclusions indicate the comparative unimportance of the spelling drill as contributory to accuracy in spelling. They suggest also that we may not only agree with Dr. Rice in his contention that more than fifteen minutes daily spelling drill is time thrown away, but may go farther than he felt warranted in going, and dispense with the spelling drill altogether without prejudice to the educational interests of the pupils." (Pp. 44 and 45.)

"ARITHMETICAL ABILITIES," by Dr. Cliff Winfield Scott, a dissertation for the Ph.D. at Columbia University:

"So far as the author is aware, the only previous comprehensive attempt to determine and account for arithmetical abilities is that of Dr. Rice. While, as will be pointed out, there are several limitations to this study, its importance can hardly be overestimated. Previous to it, practice was almost entirely based on opinion; and the success of practice was almost entirely judged by the enthusiasm of those who defended their opinions." (P. 95.)

"Environment probably has little effect on arithmetical abilities. Of the five highest systems, the majority of pupils of one came from a crowded tenement district, those of two from exceptionally good homes, and those of two from fair. Practically the same distribution is found among the five systems standing lowest." (P. 44.)

"As anything less than .25 indicates little relationship and the average of the averages of these coefficients is only .176, there is little relationship indicated between the time expended by these twenty-six systems and the abilities produced." (P. 59.)

"The greatest need shown by the research is standards of achievement. That the great variability herein shown would exist if school authorities possessed adequate means of measuring products is inconceivable; and it is believed that the present study will help standardize the work in arithmetic for the first six grades. Anyone who wishes may know how his system or school compares with the representative systems of the country." (P. 90.)

CONTENTS

SCIENTIFIC MANAGEMENT IN EDUCATION

I

EDUCATIONAL RESEARCH [1]

ALTHOUGH many of the problems concerned in elementary education have confronted the world for centuries, and many great thinkers and practical educators have endeavored to aid in their solution, the entire field is still involved in uncertainty and indefiniteness. We have opinions innumerable, but no facts are at hand in support of our opinions. Educators are divided into creeds; and while the members of the same creed are frequently in harmony with one another, and sometimes form a mutual admiration society, there are few points on which the different creeds themselves agree.

It may be said, therefore, without any exaggeration, that up to the present time the science of pedagogy has been in its entirety a structure based on no stronger foundation than one of opinions. In this regard pedagogy represents a remarkably anomalous condition; for, as the department that points the way to the development of the sciences,

[1] July-September, 1902.

it has itself failed to adopt what it has long been recommending to other scientific pursuits, namely, the inductive method of study. Its works consist of opinions, of reviews of opinions, and of opinions based on opinions, and therefore of a mass of contradictory material; and no really sustained forward movement may be expected until the conflicting views are subjected to analysis in the light of clear and unmistakable facts.

In view of the circumstance that during its long period of existence pedagogy has established no facts, that side by side with it, in other fields, facts have multiplied and developed into sciences, it is perfectly legitimate to ask whether pedagogy will admit of purely scientific treatment, whether it is possible for us to accumulate such facts as will lead to the discovery of certain fundamental pedagogical laws and certain methods and processes upon which all educators must agree.

Those who have never looked upon the educational problem from this rather novel standpoint will instinctively answer the question in the negative. They will say that the problem is complicated by so many elements which enter into the development of the child mind that no definite conclusions can be drawn. They will be supported in this view by the fact that even broad-minded teachers of wide experience differ on the most elementary points coming under their daily observation. And this further item may be mentioned in their favor, that even the same teachers are continually changing their views, that they no longer believe in one year what they firmly believed the year before, and that a year later they will begin to feel that their second theory was wrong and the first was right, and so on indefinitely.

The evidence in favor of the negative side, though exceedingly strong, is, however, not at all conclusive. That in spite of all efforts the whole field of pedagogy should be still so very indefinite proves without doubt that, as a whole, the problem is a complicated one; but it does not prove that we have availed ourselves of all possible means that may be of service in its solution. It may be that the nature of the child mind is so elusive, and the influence of natural endowment, heredity, and environment so varied, that all definite observation is rendered impossible. Or, on the other hand, it may be that we have not yet applied the proper methods of observation. If the former is true, we shall have to abandon the idea of ever developing a real science of pedagogy, and continue to grope our way in the dark. If, on the other hand, the latter is the case, then we must see what can be done to improve our methods of observation.

In my opinion, both propositions may be answered in the affirmative, and this for the reason that the problem of elementary education presents two distinct phases, one of which is involved in subtleties and belongs to the department of philosophy, while the other is much more superficial, and is, in large part, a question of science. Each one of these phases has its special goals, and each its special means of reaching those goals. The trouble lies in the fact that the two sides have never been properly discriminated. The first includes all those factors which relate to the development of character, while the other is concerned with the acquisition of knowledge and skill.

Broadly speaking, the means employed in the development of character—the will, the tastes, the habits, the feelings—are represented by the course of study as a whole, and concern the question of what the schools shall teach, the branches, and to a certain extent the material in each branch. As the composite picture of what the future man or woman should be differs in different individuals and is a matter of philosophical creed, the broader aims of the elementary schools will always differ more or less in accordance with creeds. Therefore, in countries, such as the United States, where individual communities are free to conduct their own schools as they choose, the courses of study will continue to differ in different localities, and will represent the nature of the inhabitants, the stamp of the members of the school board, and the individual opinions of the superintendent.

The means employed in the acquisition of knowledge and skill, on the other hand, represent the elements involved in carrying out the mandates of the course of study, and are matters of detail in school work. They include the division of the material of each branch into parts suitable for each grade, the amount of time to be devoted to each subject in each grade, the methods of teaching each subject, etc. Although this aspect of the problem, as well as the other, has been thus far treated from the standpoint of creed, it is not a matter of creed, but one of scientific inquiry, and calls for treatment on the inductive plan. That it constitutes the heart of the problem of practical pedagogy, and merits careful consideration on the part of all thinking people, I shall endeavor to make clear during the course of this chapter.

On the practical side of school work, two questions are always before us: (1) How much time shall be devoted to a subject? and (2) what results shall be accomplished? These two questions have been discussed *ad nauseam* in pedagogical works and at educational meetings; but educators are no nearer to an agreement at present than they have ever been. The difficulty is that they have never taken into consideration that there is a relation between the two questions. They have simply tried to answer them independently, and on a basis of philosophical creed. In consequence, we have a mass of philosophical opinion as to what results shall be accomplished in each branch, and a mass of philosophical opinion as to how much time shall be devoted to each branch. And there the matter ends.

Now as the ship of pedagogy, with respect to these two questions, has become waterlogged in a sea of opinions, efforts should be made to point the ship in a different direction and find whether we cannot get out of the trough. In this case, the matter is a very simple one: it is merely necessary to change the form of the proposition in order to be able to forge ahead. Instead of stating what results shall be accomplished, let us ask, "What results can we get?" This changes the position of the educator from a dogmatic one to one of scientific inquiry. It opens the way to investigations which will enable us to learn what results the schools of our country have been getting—the good, the moderate, and the poor—and therefore what results may be reasonably expected. Our demands may then be stated in very definite terms. The results demanded are reasonable results.

As to the amount of time to be devoted to a subject, the answer is, "A reasonable amount of time to get reasonable results." To arrive at a conclusion in this matter we must find how much time has been given to a subject in the schools where reasonable results have been obtained, and make our calculations accordingly.

The element of time is the saving clause. If we were to demand results alone, we should be in danger of going back to the methods employed in the old-fashioned, mechanical schools. But this cannot occur when we limit the time in which the prescribed results must be secured; for if more than a reasonable time is absorbed in accomplishing the demanded results, the school is below the standard.

It is clear that the plan of measuring results in units of time is limited in application. It cannot be applied at all to abstract qualities represented by traits of character, and perhaps not to certain phases of knowledge and skill; but it can be very readily applied to spelling, penmanship, language, and arithmetic—the branches to which, on the average, about seventy per cent of the school time is now devoted. I base this claim not on mere opinion, but on actual investigation.

The plan of application is very simple. It lies in subjecting children taught under different systems to one and the same test—which must be fair and practical—and comparing the results. Each branch requires a special treatment of its own. In spelling, words are dictated to the children in columns and sentences. In arithmetic, a set of questions covering such work as is undertaken in all schools is given. In language, a story is read to the children, and the pupils reproduce it in their own words. The penmanship may form a part of the test in language. The papers will show the legibility and neatness of the handwriting, etc.

By subjecting the pupils of the schools of different cities to the same test in any one branch to which the plan is applicable, we can, without doubt, get at the comparative standing of different cities in that branch, and substitute facts for opinions in regard to whether or not the teachers of those cities have been successful in the teaching of that branch. If in arithmetic, for instance, the questions are so selected, grade for grade, that no exception is taken to them by the teachers of any city, and the results show that the pupils in city A can do the examples without any difficulty while those of city B can scarcely do them at all, then the facts prove that the children in A are a great deal stronger in arithmetic than those in B, and that there is probably something radically wrong with the arithmetic in B.

At the time of writing (May, 1902), I am in the midst of a test in arithmetic; and what I have just stated is not an imaginary, but an actual, case. The differences in results in different cities are so great as to be almost incredible. In the highest grammar-school grade, for instance, the class averages have thus far ranged between eleven and ninety-one per cent. As my test consists of eight examples, this means that while in the best class examined every child was able to perform correctly more than seven problems out of the eight, in the poorest they did not average even one right to the pupil. Several of the highest grammar-school classes averaged under twenty-five per cent, while some averaged over eighty per cent. And what is true of these differences in individual classes is representative of different cities as a whole. In other words, while in some cities the percentages in general were high, in others they were extremely low. The schools were not selected, but taken at random; care being exercised simply as to neighborhood, so that the well-to-do, the middle-class, and the poor districts might all be represented.

While excellent results in city A and miserable results in city B, secured on a perfectly fair test, taken under the same conditions, will convince the average man of affairs that the children of A are stronger in arithmetic than those of B, these results do not necessarily carry the same meaning to school superintendents and teachers, who, as a class, are not supposed to be people of affairs, but philosophers and psychologists. If the pupils of A should obtain an average of ninety-five per cent, and those of B should average not more than five per cent, some educators, with pronounced opinions as to methods, would not be swerved from their belief that the pupils of city B were really the stronger, if they happened to believe in the methods used in B; and they would argue that the comparative strength in arithmetic, as between the pupils of two cities, could not be demonstrated by any test devised by man. Fortunately, however, many school superintendents are taking a much more rational view of the question than they did only a few years ago. They are really anxious to know what their pupils can do in comparison with those of other cities; they appreciate that the results obtained through my tests have an important bearing on the question; and if their pupils fail they sincerely wish to know it as well as the reasons for the failure.

For all practical purposes, then, I think we have a right to declare that we can determine how the children in different cities compare with each other in certain branches as regards results; that from this standpoint we can classify the cities into good, fair, and poor; and that we can strike an average upon which we can base a reasonable demand.

But the results alone do not tell us the whole story. They merely give us, commercially speaking, an account of the articles purchased, without indicating whether good value has been received for the capital invested. The child's capital is represented by time; and whether certain results are to be lauded or condemned depends upon the amount of time expended in obtaining them. Children in all cities have about the same amount of capital at their disposal for school purposes, three hundred minutes a day; and the practical problem lies in discovering how this capital may be expended on sound economical principles, *i.e.*, without waste.

Applying this principle to arithmetic, it might be said that, if the cities devoting sixty minutes a day to the subject should secure a general average of sixty per cent, while those giving only forty minutes should obtain an average of forty per cent, all these children were receiving equal value for the capital expended. It would then become debatable whether it was well to spend one-fifth of the capital on arithmetic, or whether it was advisable to be content with less of that branch and devote part of the sixty minutes to some other subject. But if city A with its forty minutes should obtain an average of sixty per cent, while city B with its sixty minutes should secure an average of only forty per cent, then it would be evident that, for some reason or other, the children of A were not only paying thirty-three per cent less for their arithmetic than those of B, but that for the lower price they were getting a far superior article. The actual proportion as to price stated in units would be as forty to ninety. The problem lies in finding a reasonable market price.

Now my tests, which cover schools in a large number of cities, show without any doubt whatever that educators have no idea of price, that the results bear no relation to the time expended, that some schools pay a very high price for a very poor article, and others pay a very low price for a very good article, while all sorts of prices are paid for the identical article.

For example, in my spelling test, which was taken in nineteen cities, the variations in results were small, but the time given to the subject in different cities varied from ten to forty minutes a day. Computation showed that, taken all in all, the children did not do any better where they had spent forty minutes a day on spelling than in the schools where they had spent only ten. Or, stating the matter commercially, some children were paying a dollar for an article that other children were purchasing for twenty-five cents.

In arithmetic, as I have already indicated, the variations in results have been enormous; but while they have been very good in some cities and extremely low in others, the results have borne no relation to the time given to the branch. The schools in which the children have been making a very poor showing have devoted just as much time to the subject as the schools where the problems have been solved without any difficulty, and in some instances more. The constant cry on the part of citizens for more time to spelling and more time to arithmetic is ridiculous. Whatever the shortcomings may be, the remedy does not lie in an increase of time.

What I have said in regard to the time element in teaching is in one sense a solution of the most important educational question of the day, namely, "Can the schools cover a wide range of subjects without neglecting the essentials?" If my investigations have proved any one thing, it is that time given to a subject beyond a certain point is not rewarded by additional return, that nothing can be gained by pressure; and the indications are that all the benefit that can be obtained through instruction in the formal studies—reading, spelling, penmanship, language, and arithmetic—can be had in two hours a day at the utmost. This means that we can enrich the course of study abundantly without detriment to the three R's, and that if the results are below a reasonable standard, in any locality where a reasonable amount of time is given to the formal studies, the failure is not due to a lack of amount of instruction in these branches, but to some other cause.

But when we know what results can be accomplished and the time in which reasonable results ought to be obtained, we have simply secured the needed foundation for the study of pedagogy on the inductive principle. It is not enough to know that some schools are very much more successful than others; we must also try to learn the reasons why some have succeeded and others have failed, and in this way endeavor to discover certain fundamental laws of teaching which may be applied by all. Upon this matter we are all at sea to-day. There are plenty of theories, but my investigations have proved that our preconceived notions have no foundation in fact. Many elements must be taken into consideration, such as the age, nationality, heredity, and environment of the pupils, the training and personality of the teacher, the methods of instruction, the views of the superintendent, etc. But my figures prove that the influence of these factors is to-day unknown; and unless we secure a working basis it must forever remain unknown.

For example, every one seems to take it for granted that spelling is a question of heredity; but if this is the case, how is it that the highest percentage in the United States, on my test, was secured in a school where ninety-five per cent of the pupils were children of Bohemian cigar-makers? In arithmetic, the children in the slums of some cities did a great deal better than those of the best districts in others. This does not agree with our theories of environment, at least as far as arithmetic is concerned. Then, again, if all depended on the training and personality of the teacher, we should not find good results in the large majority of instances in one locality and the opposite condition in another, while the teachers may be fully as well trained and carefully selected in the one community as in the other. Nor can the difference be accounted for on the score of methods alone; as some teachers do well with certain methods, while others completely fail with them. The size of classes must also be ruled out, the results being just as liable to be favorable in large as they are in small classes. Perhaps the demands of the superintendent play an important part; and this, again, is a point calling for most careful study. The mere fact that very good results can be obtained among children whose home surroundings are of the poorest, while very inferior results are frequently found where the conditions are all that can be desired, is sufficient evidence to upset many of our previous calculations.

Now that it has been demonstrated that we have a ready means of learning with what success each teacher is meeting, and therefore a basis for studying why certain schools are successful and others are not, there ought to be no delay in taking advantage of it. But who is to do the work, and who is to pay for it?

Among the channels that at once suggest themselves are the Bureau of Education at Washington, the departments of pedagogy in our universities, the normal schools, and the National Educational Association. Any or all of these institutions would be suitable; but they are slow in according recognition to new ideas and in carrying them to a point of practical usefulness. I do not doubt that in due course of time the work would be taken up, officially, in one little corner, by one of the bodies I have mentioned, and would leap from it to another little corner, and that in the course of twenty-five years it would be generally recognized. But why should we wait twenty-five years? Why not act at once? If the ways of red tape and philosophy are slow, who is to compel us to employ these agencies?

But who is to further the work if not these established institutions? Why, those who are most directly interested in the schools, the people themselves. In this matter our country is fortunately situated; for the people of each community own their own schools and are free to conduct them as they choose, so that they need not wait for the good-will of others if they desire to branch out in any progressive direction. The plan is practical and its effects are immediate, and it is therefore one for the practical people to take in hand. The people as a whole are not interested in pedagogy, because they do not understand it, and they are not in sympathy with pedagogues, because they do not understand their subtle minds. But the people are intensely interested in the schools, for the support of which they are willing to dip down into their pockets to almost any depth, with reverence, and, as a rule, without the slightest murmur. That they have never taken an intelligent interest in the schools is not their fault, but that of the educators themselves; for how can they be expected to distinguish the true from the false when the leaders in the profession do not agree as to which is the one and which the other? The system I recommend is intelligible to all; and if it should be carried into effect, laymen could take a really intelligent interest in their schools. It would give them an opportunity of knowing what returns they were getting for the capital expended, because it would enable them to learn with what success each individual teacher was meeting as compared with that of other teachers. Even people who spend money lavishly are anxious to make the best bargain for what they do spend.

Now, any community can carry out the system if the citizens are willing to pay for the special services required. While the plan is simple, it entails considerable labor; and in order that the work may be properly and systematically performed, some one must be designated to do it and to be held responsible for it. As the city superintendent has his hands full enough at present, a special office must be created for the purpose. To the superintendent, however, such assistance would be of great value. Upon him devolves the work of supervising teachers, and largely that of recommending their appointment or reappointment, of preparing courses of study, time tables for the different grades, etc.; and in all these matters the records prepared by a special assistant would be an invaluable guide. Moreover, by repeating the tests from time to time, he would have a much clearer idea of how his recommendations were working out than he can have when he shoots at random, as he now does, and there is no one to tell him when he hits or misses the target.

Besides taking tests and tabulating results, the work of the special assistant would lie in endeavoring to account for the differences in results on the part of different teachers in his locality; and it would be the duty of the special assistant in each city to work in harmony with similar assistants in other cities, in order to account for differences in results in various branches in different localities. Under these circumstances, the children could at once receive the benefit of every new discovery. The small additional expense involved in maintaining an office of this kind should not be considered any more than people consider whether, by reason of expense, their school halls shall be illuminated with candles or electric lights. If one enterprising city will take the initiative, others will be sure to follow, just as others followed the leader in engaging a city superintendent.

My plan of investigation first appeared in print in my article on "Obstacles to Rational Educational Reform," which was published in *The Forum* for December, 1896, and which is Chapter II of this book; and in a way that I had not anticipated I brought it directly to the notice of the Department of Superintendence at its annual meeting in Indianapolis, in February, 1897. I had been invited to conduct a round-table discussion on the three R's, and had expected a handful of people to talk the matter over quietly and leisurely. But it so happened that the round-table turned out to be a mass meeting, including the picked educational people of the country. After a few opening remarks, I endeavored to arouse discussion on a question which I stated somewhat as follows: In some cities ten minutes a day are devoted to spelling for eight years; in others, forty. Now how can we tell at the end of eight years whether the children who have had forty minutes are better spellers than those who have had only ten?

I had expected, in this way, to draw out the ideas of those who believed in much teaching of spelling and those who believed in little of it, and thus to labor for a compromise; but, to my great surprise, the question threw consternation into the camp. The first to respond was a very popular professor of psychology engaged in training teachers in the West. He said, in effect, that the question was one that could never be answered; and he gave me a rather severe drubbing for taking up the time of such an important body of educators in asking them silly questions.

The next speaker was a prominent superintendent, who did not like the way I had been treated and tried to come to my rescue. After this, quite a number took the platform in response to calls from the audience, and spoke on spelling in a general way; but no one attempted to answer the question.

Then followed comments among the audience which were anything but flattering to me. There was a general agreement that my meeting had been a failure. I heard one remark to the effect that the afternoon had been wasted. Another accused me of trying to lead the superintendents into a trap. The only comments which seemed to run contrary to the current were those of a well-known superintendent, who said to me, " I am not quite sure that the meeting was so very much of a failure," and of another, who said, with a smile, "We don't know anything."

After the meeting of the superintendents in 1897, the question of educational results was not, to my knowledge, again brought before them until five years later (February, 1902), when Dr. Paul H. Hanus, Professor of Education at Harvard University, came out in the strongest terms in support of the same idea. Professor Hanus's paper was published, somewhat modified, in *The Forum* for April, 1902, under the title "Our Chaotic Education"; and to show the firm position taken by him in regard to the matter, I shall quote the following passages:

No physicist or biologist would ignore his fellow-workers in this way. When Roentgen announced his discovery, other physicists confirmed his discovery. The facts of embryology and their bearing on the theory of evolution are similarly confirmed by each biologist under the conditions which led to their discovery. The principles of science once established in this way, no one can doubt or belittle them. Each experimenter then sees clearly what conditions must be observed to secure certain results, and the application of principles proceeds intelligently, no matter how varied the circumstances under which the application is made. So it must be in education, if we are ever to escape from the quagmire of random and isolated experimenting in which each worker seeks to find the way out for himself, disregarding the landmarks and sign-posts that have already been set up by his predecessors. Briefly, then, we must organize our educational experience just as we must organize our educational doctrine, if we are to make real progress.

Under such circumstances we could face the teaching profession and the general public with facts, instead of opinions. The enormous difference between the weight of these two very different things in educational affairs still remains to be experienced. . . .

The only comprehensive attempt known to the writer to secure definite information concerning the actual achievement of the schools in the school arts, with a view to establishing just how much time can be saved by suitable restriction and selection of subject-matter, was made by the editor of *The Forum.* His investigations would naturally be of great importance for any future researches that might be undertaken.

The articles referred to were published in *The Forum* for December, 1896, and January, February, April, and June, 1897, being Chapters II-VI of the present work.

II

OBSTACLES TO RATIONAL EDUCATIONAL REFORM [1]

THE purpose of the present article is to point out how, in my opinion, the obstacles to rational educational progress may be overcome, and the cooperation secured on the part of all forces toward the development of an ideal system of schools.

While in former years I entertained the belief, in common with others, that the cause of the obstacles to educational progress might be attributed to public indifference and its consequences—politics in school boards, incompetent supervision, insufficient preparation on the part of teachers, etc.—further study and reflection have led me to the conclusion that these elements are not the ultimate cause of the evil, but constitute only the symptoms of a much more deeply hidden disease which permits all sorts of havoc to be played with the schools. The evil to which I refer is this; namely, that educators themselves cannot come to an agreement in regard to what changes, if any, are desirable or feasible. Many educators—men of learning and experience—do not appear to be in sympathy with the system of education advocated by reformers. Others, while admiring the spirit of the so-called "new education," ques-

[1] December, 1896.

tion the feasibility of carrying out its demands in the common schools. Last, the great mass of our teachers, who have not entered into the intricacies of the problem, finding that there are many sides to the question, are in a state of doubt, ready to be led by any faction.

The ultimate cause of the lamentably slow progress toward the introduction of educational reforms may be traced, therefore, beyond the province of the general public, into the professional circle itself; to an inner strife and turmoil consequent upon the uncertainties in which the entire problem of elementary education is involved. Consequently, in my opinion, the fate of educational reform rests entirely in the hands of educators, and will be decided by what is done, through their efforts, to dispel the uncertainties which have led the public to hesitate. In other words, if the educators can be brought to an understanding, the obstructions from without will take care of themselves. But is it possible for all educators to meet on a common ground and together lay out definite plans of action?

If the source of the difficulty could be traced to a material difference in point of view in regard to the purpose of elementary education—what, under ideal conditions, the elementary schools of our country ought to accomplish—then of course, endeavors to bring the various educational factions to an agreement would be as fruitless as endeavors to secure religious unity. A careful consideration of educational discussions, however, shows that a difference of opinion on the general purpose of our schools does not exist; for there is substantially an agreement to the effect that the general aim of the elementary schools of our country is to develop a moral individual, endowed with the power of independent thought, the ability to earn an honest livelihood, culture, refinement, and a broad and intelligent interest in human affairs. As the source of the conflict cannot be traced to the problem of educational purposes, we cannot fail to conclude that it must be sought at the practical end of the problem. And it is here that the difficulty actually lies. For, while we are agreed that the ultimate purpose of elementary education is to develop a good citizen, in the broadest sense of the term, we are by no means clear in regard to what to do, in order that the child may receive the benefit of all that can be done for him.

In matters pertaining to the practical conduct of the schools, our notions to-day are not much more definite than they might have been a century ago. Indeed, so crude are they that no sooner do we dip beneath the surface in our inquiries than we find ourselves surrounded by utter confusion. The statements made on practical questions, even among our leading educators, are conflicting to the point of absurdity. And, as there are no proofs to offer as to who is right and who is wrong, we are left completely without a guide; so that we do not know which way to turn. Everything is speculative: nothing is positive. "I think" and "I believe" are the stereotyped expressions of the educational world: "I know" has not yet been admitted. If our ideas on the practical side should be vague only in regard to certain subtle questions now under discussion in our leading pedagogical circles, and involving hair-breadth metaphysical distinctions, the weaknesses would certainly be pardonable. Perfection cannot be found in any department of learning. But the complexion becomes entirely changed when we consider that we have absolutely no definite knowledge in regard to the most elementary questions; that our ideas in regard to a proper treatment of the old subjects—reading, spelling, penmanship, grammar, composition, and arithmetic—are fully as indefinite as they are in regard to what course to pursue in the sciences and the arts, or in the training of the moral character. Our leading educators are not even agreed, for example, as to whether the results secured by a five-year course in technical grammar are better than those secured by a one-year course, or whether the results will not be just as good if technical grammar be entirely omitted from the elementary schools. And, again, they are by no means agreed as to whether or not children who devote forty minutes daily to spelling turn out to be better spellers than those who devote, say, not more than five or ten minutes daily to that subject.

The element which, above all others, leads our people to doubt the feasibility of the new education concerns the problem as to whether or not there is enough "time" at our disposal to secure satisfactory results in reading, writing, and arithmetic, if new subjects be freely introduced into the schools. In view of what I have just stated; namely, that the opinions of the most experienced vary enormously on the question of the time required to do a piece of work, it may readily be seen that whatever may be said on the subject at present is merely a random guess. Many of our reformers have endeavored to evade this question altogether by arguments to the effect that the three R's are merely the tools of knowledge, and that, consequently, they are of much less educative value than the matters on which the new education lays stress. But such arguments will not aid the cause; for, whatever our individual notions on the point at issue may be, we cannot escape from the fact that the citizen who is not properly grounded in the three R's labors at a disadvantage in the struggle for existence, so that duty compels us to check our individual inclinations and to bow gracefully to the inevitable.

Until the truth is known concerning the possibility of broadening the curriculum without detriment to the three R's, educational conflict will not abate, and the road to progress will continue to be barred. Therefore, the work which, above all others, ought now to engage the attention of our people, in order that the children may receive the benefit of all that it is possible to do for them, is to undertake measures that will lead to the positive discovery as to how much time is actually required to secure satisfactory results in reading, writing, and arithmetic. That to-day we are utterly unable to give an intelligent answer to this question is due simply to the fact that we have not yet made an attempt to discover the landmark which must serve as a guide in directing our judgment. And, before we shall be able to make any progress in the solution of this problem, it will be necessary definitely to locate the central point around which the entire problem of educational reform revolves. The landmark to which I refer is simply this: namely, a clear definition of what is meant by the term "satisfactory results." If we do not know what we mean by satisfactory results, how shall we be able, with any degree of intelligence, to judge when our task has been satisfactorily performed? If we have no definite goal, who can tell how long it will take to reach it, or what road will most directly lead to it? Until we come to a definite understanding in regard to this matter, our entire educational work will lack direction, and we shall continue, as heretofore, to grope our way along passages completely enveloped in darkness, in an endeavor to land we know not where.

If we might have a standard which would enable us to tell when our task had been completed, our attention might be earnestly directed toward the discovery of short cuts in educational processes, which would enable the child, by the expenditure of very little time, to acquire the demanded knowledge and skill in branches whose educative value is small. Thus, by securing a standard of measurement for determining the results in the three R's alone, our progressive educators might become freed from the fetters of prejudice, to labor, without restraint, toward the realization of higher ideals. Moreover, in the branches that are distinctively educative, a definite goal is necessary in order to determine the feasibility of certain methods of instruction. How, for example, will it be possible to determine whether or not satisfactory results can be secured in history and geography, if these subjects be unified in instruction, unless we have an understanding in regard to what is meant by satisfactory results in these branches? Or, how shall we be able to tell to what extent arithmetic may be successfully taught in connection with other branches, unless we know what is meant by satisfactory results in arithmetic?

When a standard is recognized in regard to the knowledge and skill which the child ought to possess in spelling, reading, penmanship, language, arithmetic, and so on, then all teachers may benefit from the labors of others directed toward the discovery of both economical and interesting methods of teaching. For want of such a standard, each individual teacher has, thus far, been a law unto himself; permitted to experiment on his pupils in accordance with his own individual educational notions, whether inherited from his grandmother or the result of study and reflection, entirely regardless of what was being done by others. So long as this condition is possible, pedagogy cannot lay claim to recognition as a science. In the recognized fields of science, such as physics, chemistry, medicine, etc., the members of the profession are not only willing to learn from each other, but they are compelled to do so under penalty of the law. Those who fail, in practice, to give due recognition to important discoveries are held responsible for the consequences. Before pedagogy can be recognized as a science, it will be necessary to discover at least some truths in regard to educational processes which, if ignored by the teacher, will make him fully as liable to prosecution for malpractice as the physician who has bungled in setting a bone. Until an accurate standard of measurement is recognized by which such truths may be discovered, ward politicians will continue to wield the baton, and educational anarchy will continue to prevail.

It may here be argued that it would be impossible to secure a definite standard for measuring results, generally applicable in our country, on the ground that the needs of our people vary in different localities. While this sentiment deserves recognition, it will become apparent, during the course of this chapter, that proper attention to local conditions, in the conduct of our elementary schools, would not tend in the least to alter the plan as a whole.

At present, our ideas in regard to what the elementary schools are in duty bound to accomplish, or how much may be reasonably expected of the pupil, do not extend beyond a few very general notions. There is an agreement, first, that the child, on leaving school, should be able to read; second, that he should possess the ability to write a letter or a composition in a neat, legible hand, without mistakes in spelling, grammar, or punctuation; third, that he should be skilled in the use of figures; fourth, that he should have some knowledge of geography; and, fifth, that he should know some history. That we have no definite standard, however, in any one of these branches, becomes apparent so soon as we seek for definite information. How many and which words should the child be able to spell, on leaving school, without referring to a dictionary? Ought our citizen to be a *littérateur*, or will the ability to write a good English sentence be satisfactory? Shall the child's penmanship, on graduating from the elementary school, be of sufficient elegance to enable him to earn money by writing visiting cards, or will a legible hand suffice? A very important question that arises in connection with this apparently insignificant subject concerns a definition of what is meant by a legible hand. How far-reaching this matter actually is may be seen when we consider that the desire to secure an elegant instead of a neat handwriting may exert a great influence on the *entire school course.* The extra amount of time required in travelling from legibility to elegance might be, in itself, sufficient to crowd nature-study out of the curriculum. Moreover, the desire to secure elegant penmanship might necessitate a movement so slow in everything that the child was obliged to write as to interfere seriously with his development in other directions. Again, shall the child, when he graduates from the elementary school, be able, on demand, to solve any arithmetical puzzle that any one may choose to place before him? Or, last, shall he be able, on call, to rattle off the boundaries of Ethiopia? If not, where shall the limit be drawn?

For lack of a definite standard, the selection of material for instruction has been made, thus far, in an arbitrary way, under no control other than that of tradition and individual opinion. The old-fashioned schoolmaster's method of procedure has been by far the easiest. His plan has been to set aside a certain number of hours each week for instruction in a given subject, and, during that time, to crowd into the child's mind as many things as possible, in the hope that some of them will be remembered, but without any particular regard for the question as to what good they would do even if they should happen to be retained. The new school of educators, on the other hand, has endeavored to solve the problem by selecting material that will interest the child, whereby much has been done to relieve the work of needless drudgery. But this method, also, has failed to give satisfaction; for, while the reformers have criticized the old-fashioned system as wasteful, in so far as too many useless facts are taught, the criticism passed on the new plan of work has been that it is too indefinite, and that, in consequence, it destroys the backbone of the old system without putting anything definite in its place. That so much conflict should exist in regard to what ought to be accomplished in each branch is not due to the fact that there is no guide which will enable us to determine what is our duty. It is simply due to the fact that, for want of research in the proper direction, our notions on the subject have never become clear. When the matter is regarded in its proper light, it will be seen that, in solving the problem "What to teach," the individual educator is not entirely free to choose, but that, within certain limits, the matter is governed by definite laws. By reason of the fact that, within the prescribed limits, the same laws apply to all alike, a study of the laws which govern this matter would enable us to find a standard of measurement on which all our educators might agree.

The law by which the selection of material is governed is represented, at least in part, by the demands of society for a definite amount of positive knowledge and skill. That we cannot agree in regard to what must be done is due simply to the fact that we are not properly acquainted with what is needed. Consequently, the work which, above all other, should now absorb the attention of our educators is that work which will lead to definite information in regard to what is required, and how much can be expected of the child, in individual branches of knowledge. When our ideas on this matter are clear, it will be possible to secure a selection of material that will be no longer provided in an arbitrary way, but will be such as to satisfy the demands of all. When we are clear in regard to what is needed, it will be possible to determine what results in individual branches may be deemed satisfactory, and how much time will be required to reach this goal. By securing an agreement in regard to what must be accomplished by all, the educator would not be deprived of his individuality. On the contrary, he would be much more free than he has ever been; for, so long as the demanded results were obtained, he would be at liberty both to present the desired material in any form that he might choose and to do as much else as he might deem fit. How the necessary data which would lead to definite conclusions on this subject might be secured will be pointed out later on.

The establishment of a standard to enable the teacher to tell when his task in a given branch has been satisfactorily performed constitutes only one of the practical problems with which the educator is confronted. The remaining problem is concerned in the discovery of a standard by which may be determined how much time it is necessary to devote to a subject in order to complete this task. By the establishment of such a standard, we should be given a basis for testing the comparative economy of different educational processes. That the importance of labor in this direction cannot be overestimated becomes apparent when we consider that the extent to which the child's education may be broadened depends almost entirely upon the time required to secure satisfactory results in reading, writing, and arithmetic. That, at present, we are absolutely unable to form an intelligent judgment in regard to how much time ought to be consumed in completing a piece of work is proved by what has already been stated; namely, that educators are not even agreed as to whether better spellers will be produced by devoting forty minutes daily to spelling than by devoting not more than five or ten minutes daily to that subject; or whether the results secured by a five-year course in technical grammar are superior to those obtained by a one-year course.

Our lack of knowledge on this point, however, is not due to the fact that nothing positive can be known in regard to the comparative economy of different educational processes. It is due simply to the fact that the proper steps have not yet been taken which will give us the required information. That educators should thus far have failed to throw the needed light on the subject may be fully explained by the fact that they have endeavored to solve the problem by means of hypotheses based on psychology, whereas facts alone can tell the tale. In a word, they have made the fatal mistake of exactly reversing the true order of things. Instead of proving the accuracy of their hypotheses by a study of the results of a given process, they have endeavored to prove, in advance, what the results of methods based on these hypotheses must be. The plight into which this mode of procedure has brought us will become obvious by a simple illustration.

For example, psychology will permit one to argue that ideas will not be clear unless they have absorbed the entire attention for a time. This would indicate that, in arranging a school programme, it was necessary to set aside a certain period—entirely arbitrary, however—to be devoted to instruction in spelling. On the other hand, we are as fully justified in reasoning that in school the child is obliged to devote a considerable amount of time to writing; that whenever he writes he spells; and that, in consequence, it is not necessary to provide any special time on the programme for spelling. Which of these two methods of reasoning is correct can be determined only by a study of results.

That general psychology, in itself, should fail to

be of direct assistance in determining the question of economy of effort is due to the fact that this subject is purely a qualitative science, treating of the qualities of the mind, while economy of effort in teaching is strictly a quantitative problem. Psychology teaches us the laws in accordance with which the mind digests ideas; but it gives us no information whatever in regard to the number of ideas that can be digested within a given period, or how much time is required to complete the digestion of a given number of ideas.

To illustrate: We learn from psychology that the concrete precedes the abstract. This has led many to believe, for instance, that in the early lessons in arithmetic the child should handle objects, in order that he may secure a clear conception of the meaning of numbers. But how many hours of the child's school time ought to be consumed in acquiring a clear conception of numbers up to ten cannot be learned from psychology, being purely a question of experience. Again, as I have already stated, we are all agreed that when the child has completed his elementary school course he ought to be able to write an ordinary letter without gross mistakes in grammar. But what amount of time must be devoted to technical grammar in order to accomplish this result; whether it will necessitate a five-year course, or a one-year course, or whether it can be accomplished simply through incidental hints—these are questions upon which the most learned dissertations on the origin and psychology of language cannot throw any light whatever. There is only one method by which such matters can be determined, which is that of discovering how much time has been consumed by the most successful teachers in reaching a certain end. It is only in this way that we shall be able to learn how much time it is necessary to consume in order to complete a given piece of work, and, again, to discover which particular educational processes will serve to accomplish a given task by the expenditure of the smallest amount of time.

What must be done, then, in order that our system of education may be placed on a secure foundation is to institute researches toward obtaining facts that will lead, first, to the establishment of standards by which the teacher may be able to determine when his task in a given branch has been satisfactorily performed; and, secondly, to the establishment of standards which will enable us to judge how much time is needed to secure a definite result. Once these truths are recognized, the factional lines between conservatives and radicals will cease to exist, and all will become co-laborers in the discovery of the laws that apply to all our educators, regardless of pedagogical creed.

In order to test the feasibility of researches such as I have outlined, I have devoted the past two years to examining children taught by every conceivable method, in schools representing a very large section of our country. By means of examinations in a number of school branches—spelling, penmanship, English composition, and arithmetic—I hoped to be able, first, to establish certain goals through the discovery of what our children might reasonably be expected to accomplish; and, secondly, by a comparison of results, to arrive at some definite conclusions concerning the comparative economy of different methods of teaching. The number of children examined has thus far reached nearly one hundred thousand; and care was exercised to secure exact information, not only in regard to the methods employed, but also in regard to the age, nationality, and environment of the children, in order that the influence of conditions might be duly taken into consideration. These examinations have brought some things to light, which, in my opinion, are destined to destroy many of our preconceived notions. The results will be published in detail during the course of this work.

The labor involved in taking the tests, in marking the papers, and in the preparation of the very elaborate statistical tables has been so great as to require the undivided attention of myself and a number of special assistants. Although for individual enterprise the undertaking may be considered as almost unwieldy, I have become fully convinced, as the result of my researches, that, by means of concerted efforts on the part of teachers, or by the establishment of a bureau supported by our National Government, not only would the work become comparatively simple, but it would lead to the very speedy solution of a number of vital educational questions, and would thus serve, in a comparatively brief period, to place our schools on a rational foundation. Moreover a study of this nature would lead, inductively, to the development of an educational psychology, of which we have long been speaking, but which, in fact, does not yet exist.

In closing, I desire once more to emphasize the point that the plan proposed in this chapter would not lead to the destruction of the individuality of the teacher, but that, on the contrary, it would mean a degree of individual freedom far beyond any that has been hitherto enjoyed. While the necessity for completing a definite task in each school branch is recognized, nothing is contained in the plan that would interfere with the employment of any pedagogical scheme, or with the development of the child in any direction, so long as the teacher would be able, by her methods, to secure the stipulated results. And, in my opinion, it is not until the standards that I have pointed out shall have been established that we shall have an intelligent basis upon which to construct a course of study, or to apportion the time in the arrangement of a school programme, or to form the slightest conception concerning the possibilities of elementary education.

III

THE ESSENTIALS IN ELEMENTARY EDUCATION [1]

In the preceding chapter I discussed the possibility of securing satisfactory results in the so-called essentials if the course of study in the elementary schools were materially enriched. I argued that nothing definite could now be said on this subject, because no agreement had yet been reached, either in regard to what is essential, or as to what results in individual branches may be deemed satisfactory. Until our ideas are clear on these matters, we shall of course be unable to estimate how much time it is necessary to devote to the formal studies, and how much should be set aside for work that is purely educative in its nature.

Before it will be possible to decide how far the curriculum may be safely broadened, then, two questions will have to be answered much more satisfactorily than has been thus far the case. In the first place, it will be necessary to arrive at a much clearer understanding as to which of the things commonly taught in the elementary schools are in fact essential, and which of them could be eliminated without material detriment to the child; and, secondly, it will be incumbent upon us to establish standards that

[1] January, 1897

will serve as guides in enabling us to tell how much time is required to cover satisfactorily the indispensable ground. In the present chapter, I shall try to throw some light on the first of these questions, while the next will be devoted to a discussion of the second.

In endeavoring to define the legitimate limits of the positive knowledge and skill that may be regarded as essential, a process of exclusion will be required. It will be necessary to exclude, first, matters belonging to the category of mental gymnastics, *i.e.*, measures introduced into the school course solely with a view to the development of the faculties, and, secondly, matters of detail that the layman is not expected to possess in the form of ready knowledge, and which are found in the school course simply because they have been handed down by tradition.

At present the time devoted to the three R's alone, in the mechanical schools, is about 70 per cent. It might be possible, however, through a process of exclusion such as I have indicated, to reduce this time by 50 per cent or more. Indeed, so great might be the change brought about that what is now regarded as the body of the work of the elementary school might, perhaps, become merely a side issue. If this should be true, then naturally the possibilities of enriching the course of study would be almost unlimited. Moreover, the exclusion of unnecessary material would form only one part of the reduction in time. An equal reduction might be secured by an exercise of economy in actual teaching—a subject that will be discussed in the next chapter.

As I have drawn a line between the essentials in a course of study and measures of educational discipline, it may be thought that I do not appreciate the value of the latter. This, however, is by no means the case. My reason for making the distinction is that, while I am of the opinion that the people are fully justified in demanding certain results in matters of useful knowledge and skill, I believe that in questions of educational discipline no universal course should be laid down, but that considerable freedom should be allowed to the exercise of judgment on the part of individual educators. The problem of mental gymnastics is still so completely veiled in obscurity, and opinions among educators in regard to the relative values of disciplinary measures vary so markedly, that dogmatism is entirely unjustifiable.

While some educators believe that the most valuable disciplinary work lies in pushing the formal branches of study beyond a reasonable point, others are of the opinion that the disciplinary value of the formal studies is far inferior to that involved in *content* studies; and that, in consequence, the time not devoted to instruction in what is actually indispensable, in the formal lines, should be devoted to such branches as the arts, the sciences, history, and literature—subjects having a direct influence in developing æsthetic taste, as well as interest in nature and humanity. It follows, therefore, that while the individual educator oversteps the limits of his authority when he fails to give due recognition to the conventional side of education, the people overstep their authority when they needlessly condemn the child to a life of drudgery, and deprive him of elevating influences, by demanding more than their due in the way of conventionalities.

One more point requires to be mentioned before entering into the discussion of details. It may be argued that, as our ideals are not fixed, the essentials of a school course cannot be clearly defined. While it is true that the demands of society are constantly changing, and that what may now be regarded as useful knowledge may not be so regarded at some indefinite period in the future, history nevertheless proves that the process of evolution is so slow, that, if standards should be set in accordance with the demands of to-day, they would answer the purpose for many years to come. Indeed, I do not think it an exaggeration to say, that, if standards should once be fixed, the labor involved in changing them, to keep pace with the process of evolution, would be, figuratively speaking, as insignificant as that involved in repairing a building, from time to time, as required by ordinary wear and tear.

The time may arrive when every individual will be permitted to spell as he chooses. But the educator who to-day should prepare his pupils for such an era would not be entitled to encouragement. Nor are we justified in believing that the period is near at hand when neat and legible writing will be no longer regarded as a necessary accomplishment. Again, the ability to use good English and facility in handling figures will not grow out of fashion within the next decade. Taken all in all, then, whatever may be said of the evolution of pedagogical ideas, we cannot consider as serious any arguments to the effect that, because we do not know exactly what the future may bring forth, we cannot tell what should now be taught in the elementary schools.

The dividing line between positive knowledge and skill, on the one hand, and mental gymnastics, on the other, may be made clear by a simple illustration.

Society expects, for example, that the individual shall be able to write a letter in well-constructed sentences and without grammatical errors. It is not concerned, however, as to whether or not the writer is able to analyze the sentences or to parse the words in his letter. If facts should prove, beyond question, that individuals who could parse and analyze with facility were able to construct better sentences than those who were unfamiliar with technical grammar, this subject might rightly be placed among the essentials of school work. If, however, it should be proved that the English employed by those who had not stüdied technical grammar was practically as good as that employed by those who had had a thorough grounding in the subject, then it could not be regarded as essential, but would belong to the domain of mental gymnastics.

In the latter case, the question of introducing technical grammar into the school course would be purely and simply a problem of relative values, *i.e.*, a question as to whether it would pay better to devote, say, thirty minutes daily, for four or five years, to grammar, or whether more profit would be derived by devoting this time to matters of importance and interest now crowded out of many of our schools on the plea of lack of time. Whether, or in how far, it is possible to lead the child to use good English without instruction in technical grammar is an entirely different question. It is one, however, that cannot be decided by *a priori* reasoning. Nothing short of the study of results will suffice to bring the truth to light.

As in language, so in arithmetic, the question of mental gymnastics plays a prominent part. While facility in ciphering, to a certain point, is demanded of every individual, whatever is done in this branch beyond what is directly useful and practical must be regarded as disciplinary in its nature. Consequently, the question arises, whether, in the arrangement of a school programme, it is advisable to allow a certain amount of time for purely disciplinary arithmetic, or whether this time might not bring a greater return if given to matters more directly destined to elevate our social ideals.

The importance of such questions of relative values becomes strikingly apparent when we consider that thirty-five minutes a day is equivalent to an entire year out of the eight devoted to elementary education. Therefore, by economizing only a little here and there, by the exclusion of merely a part of the disciplinary measures of minor or doubtful importance—such as drill in arithmetical puzzles, in superfine penmanship, in parsing and analysis beyond what is actually needed—it might be possible to save as much as the equivalent of two school years, which might then be utilized toward enriching the course of study, without in any way neglecting the essentials. When the time wasted in reading aloud merely with a view to the development of oratorical power is taken into consideration, the estimate of two years is probably too conservative.

When the purely disciplinary elements in instruction are clearly determined, one step will have been made toward defining the limits of the indispensable. The next point will lie in a process of exclusion applied to matters of detail that lie beyond what the individual may be reasonably expected to possess in the way of ready knowledge and skill. This would mean, in large part, the elimination of many things now taught in the schools, not because they are supposed to meet any particular requirement, but simply because no concerted effort has ever been made to exclude them from the traditional course of study.

The subjects that, without harm in any direction, will bear a rigid test of exclusion are spelling and penmanship. Every moment devoted to these subjects beyond what is actually needed may be regarded as wasted. When we consider that, in spite of their lack of educational value, nearly one-fifth of the time in some of our schools is devoted to these two subjects, it becomes apparent that the importance of exercising economy in teaching these branches cannot be overestimated. In determining the ground to be covered in spelling, it is necessary simply to secure an agreement as to where the line may be drawn between words that the average individual ought to be able to spell without referring to a dictionary and those that might be safely relegated to the latter. This would lead to the omission of a very large number of words now taught in the schools and which the child may never be called upon to use.

In penmanship, it will be necessary to determine what standards of legibility may be deemed satisfactory. Owing to the importance of this subject, I beg to repeat what I stated in the preceding chapter, namely, that overattention to penmanship, for the purpose of securing elegant writing, may mean the waste, both directly and indirectly, of an enormous amount of time. As the child, during the entire school course, is obliged to do considerable writing, apart from that intended to improve his penmanship, undue slowness in the use of the pen must be regarded as a waste of time against which provision should be made.

In arithmetic, aside from the disciplinary element, the question of how much ground it is necessary to cover in order that the pupil may be sufficiently well equipped to meet the ordinary demands of life requires careful consideration. By exercising a wise process of exclusion, the course might be considerably abbreviated. It would be necessary here to make a careful distinction between those parts of arithmetic with which every one ought to be conversant, and those parts concerning the more complicated calculations belonging to special lines of business, and which need to be mastered only by the specialist.

In English, in addition to the problem of mental discipline, the question as to how high the goal should be placed comes into play. In written language, limitations that do not appear in any other subject are set by the immaturity of the child-mind. In other branches, however high the goal may be placed, there is a reasonable assurance that it will be reached, provided the instruction be thorough, and ample time be provided for the purpose. In composition, however, in establishing our aims, the powers of the child must be taken into consideration. Consequently, before instruction in this subject can be conducted without undue waste, it will be necessary to learn just what the child is able to do under the most favorable circumstances. When we have learned what the most successful teachers have accomplished, and how much time they expended in reaching their ends, we shall have a sensible basis for determining what may be reasonably expected of the child, and how much time it is wise to devote to this branch.

Complaints to the effect that the results in written language are highly unsatisfactory are commonly heard from individuals in all walks of life, and particularly from instructors in high schools and universities. As the unsatisfactory results are usually attributed to insufficient attention to the subject in the elementary schools, the demand is made that still more time be devoted to English. But if the circumstances should be such that it was impossible to lead the average child beyond a certain point, however great the pressure might be, then of course the time expended in endeavoring to do so would be wasted.

An important point to be decided before definite goals can be established is the question of literary style. When we know the average child's limitations in this direction, we shall be able to tell whether or not it will pay to spend a great deal of time in endeavoring to lead the pupil to acquire the ability to write an original story, a reproduction, or a description, in good style, on the first draft. Again, we shall be able to determine whether or not time and energy expended in rewriting will be sufficiently rewarded to warrant the teacher in compelling the child to labor over a composition until he feels that he can no longer improve it. That the pupil may be trained to appreciate good literary style when he finds it in the writings of others is quite possible; but whether he can be trained to imitate it in his own writings is an entirely different question.

Next, geography, and particularly that phase which treats of the location of places, the boundaries of states and countries, the length of rivers, the height of mountains, etc., offers a broad field for exclusion without true loss in any particular. How much waste there is in the old-fashioned method of teaching this subject becomes apparent when we consider how exceedingly little the average individual has to show, a year or two after leaving school, for the numerous hours a week, during five or six years, devoted to this study. And not only from the standpoint of economy, but for other reasons as well, would the elimination of cut-and-dried facts, that properly belong to books of reference, exert a most salutary effect. For, while geography when treated in the traditional manner is one of the most burdensome subjects in the curriculum, yet, when the matters of minor importance are excluded, and substituted by valuable ideas, it becomes converted into perhaps the broadest as well as the most interesting in the entire list of school branches. While the number of facts in topographical geography that the individual is required to know in order that he may be able to take an intelligent interest in the affairs of the world is considerable, it is, nevertheless, very small when compared with that which the child is compelled to acquire in the traditional course of instruction. Indeed, so great, in my opinion, is the discrepancy between what the child is compelled to memorize in the old-fashioned schools and what the citizen is expected to know, that I do not regard it as an exaggeration to say that the traditional course in topographical geography might be shortened by 70 or 80 per cent without neglecting what is useful.

Last, I desire to call attention to the waste in a mechanical course in history. As in geography, so in this study would the preparation of a list of facts, limited to what is helpful and what the individual may be expected to possess as ready knowledge, bring about an enormous reduction in memory material. Of course, there are many facts that the individual ought to know and that every educated person is expected to know. But just what these facts are, and how many might be excluded, without impairment, from the traditional course, are matters that have never been properly determined. By a wise substitution of historical ideas for cut-and-dried facts of minor importance, history, like geography, would be converted from a mechanical study into a most valuable and interesting one.

What is needed, then, in order that a beginning may be made toward the solution of the problem of the course of study, is to undertake measures that will speedily lead to a clear definition of the essentials. In my opinion, the most rational plan would be to place the matter in the hands of committees, appointed preferably by the National Educational Association. If committees of, say, ten members should be appointed for each branch, the labor so divided that proper attention could be paid to details, and meetings held at frequent intervals, enough might be done in a single year to clear the course of study at least of those matters that are retained simply by tradition.

In drawing conclusions in regard to what to retain and what to omit, ordinary experience would suffice to set the matter well under way. For the rest, it would be necessary to undertake researches leading to the discovery of the exact limits of our social demands. But the latter course would represent a later stage, which might be carried on in a more leisurely manner. In order that the work might be thoroughly conducted, a special appropriation should be made by the Government, to be placed at the disposal of the Association.

Besides defining the essentials, it will be necessary to secure standards that will give us a basis for judging what results in the essentials may be deemed satisfactory; and not until we have these standards can it be determined how much pressure it is advisable to put on the conventional side of school work, and which methods of teaching are the most economical in point of time. But, to obtain such standards, ordinary experience will not avail: nothing short of careful research, on a very broad basis, will supply the needed information.

In our country, where elementary education is characterized by absence of system, it is not unusual for individuals, whether educators or laymen, to examine a class on a set of questions selected in an arbitrary way, and to judge by the results whether or not the teacher has done satisfactory work. So long, however, as we have no standards, judgment based on the results of an examination, in a single room, school, or city, is not only absolutely worthless, but may mean a gross injustice in estimating both the qualifications of the teachers and the value of the methods employed by them. Under existing conditions, there is only one way in which definite information in this matter can be obtained. It is by extending a reasonable test to a large number of classes, in different localities, so that all methods and conditions may be represented, and by judging of the results on a comparative basis. In this manner we are enabled to learn what results were secured by teachers in general, which classes exceeded and which fell below the average, and how much time was consumed by different methods in securing the various results. It is only in this way that we can judge whether the results obtained in any particular class, school, or city may be regarded as satisfactory.

It was with a view to the development of standards for measuring results, as well as to discover the most economical methods of teaching, that the tests in spelling, penmanship, composition, and arithmetic, to which I have referred, were made. In penmanship and composition, it is of course a simple matter to employ tests that are universally applicable. In spelling and arithmetic, although the ground covered in different cities varies considerably in regard to details, I nevertheless found that, by exercising care, the tests might be so formulated that they would cover a common ground, and thus be suitable for the schools of any locality. In spelling, three different tests were employed. One was a column of fifty words; another consisted of sentences, fifty test words being employed in the lower, and seventy-five in the upper grades; and, third, the spelling in the composition test was examined. In arithmetic, the questions were so arranged as to fit the various grades. In penmanship, the general written work was used as a test. And, finally, in composition, I employed as a test the reproduction of a story read by the teacher to the children. This story was written specially for the purpose, and was accompanied by a picture intended to aid the children in their work. The grades examined included the fourth to the eighth school years. The results are given in detail in future chapters.

While such work as this represents only a temporary stage in the development of standards, I nevertheless believe that it will suffice to lead to definite information on the most important educational problem of the day; namely, whether or not it is possible to broaden the curriculum without detriment to the three R's. To reach a conclusion on this point, it is but necessary to learn whether or not the results in the formal studies obtained in the progressive schools compare favorably with the results in the formal lines obtained in the mechanical schools. If the pupils educated in the schools in which the bulk of the work is thoughtful and interesting should do as well in the formal studies as those brought up in the schools where the work is almost entirely formal, the feasibility of the new education would be practically proved.

Until the essentials are clearly defined, then, the question of satisfactory results must be decided on a purely comparative basis. For, so long as the ground to be covered represents a very wide area, and no discrimination is made between matters of primary and those of secondary importance, the results of an examination in a given school might be apparently so unfavorable as to convey the impression that the teaching had lacked in thoroughness, while in fact the results would compare quite favorably with those secured in other schools. By a comparative study of results, even on a much narrower basis than I have indicated, a great deal might be accomplished in a very brief period toward the solution of the problem of methods. It would simply be necessary for superintendents and teachers in nieghboring localities to coöperate in a series of tests which would show the rate of progress under different methods.

When the requirements in positive knowledge and skill are limited to a reasonable point, the ideas will have an opportunity to become more thoroughly assimilated, and definite results may be demanded. Under these circumstances, it is possible that, in the course of time, absolute standards might be developed, so that it would be no longer necessary to draw comparisons on a wide basis before reaching conclusions in regard to the qualifications of a particular teacher or the excellence of a particular school.

IV

ECONOMY OF TIME IN TEACHING[1]

Having shown in the preceding chapter how considerable waste might be eliminated in the elementary schools through the exclusion of matters that did not appear to answer any definite purpose, I shall, in the present chapter, endeavor to point out what might be done toward the elimination of waste in actual teaching; thus providing still further opportunity for the introduction of purely educative material.

Of course, until an understanding is reached as to what is indispensable in an elementary-school course, and our goals are established accordingly, the study of the time element in teaching will be to some extent hampered. Nevertheless, the problem presents special features of its own that admit of separate consideration.

The point at issue involves the discovery of processes which, other things being equal, will perform a given task in the smallest amount of time. As reliable information of this nature can be obtained only by comparing results, the problem will bear solution only in so far as results can be approximately measured. Having no means at hand with

[1] February, 1897.

which to measure general intellectual strength, we are not able definitely to determine what methods of intellectual training will accomplish most in a given period; so that the relative economy of measures of mental gymnastics must remain, at least for the near future, purely a matter of speculation. Positive knowledge and skill, however, being directly amenable to measurement, it lies within our reach to ascertain the time consumed by different teachers in obtaining certain positive results, as well as to discover what processes have proved the most economical. That, in spite of our extended experience with a great variety of methods, this problem is still awaiting solution is due to the fact that the results of our experiments have never been so utilized as to lead to the discovery of scientific truths.

The fundamental points in the time element in teaching to which I shall direct particular attention are: (1) the limits of incidental instruction; (2) the influence of fatigue; and (3) the question of mental maturity.

Of these factors, that of incidental teaching is, under existing conditions, perhaps the most important. About 70 per cent of the time in some of our schools being devoted to the formal branches, a radical change would be effected if the forms of expression—reading, spelling, penmanship, grammar, and language—were taught as incidental features. Indeed, much would be gained if results should prove that the formal studies could be subordinated, even if to a limited extent only, to the content studies. The possibility of incidental instruction depends upon whether or not we are able to do more than one thing well at a time. If so, then some mental labor must necessarily be performed by subordinate states of attention or consciousness, and the practicability of incidental instruction will depend upon whether such can be utilized in teaching. That the performance of more than one act at a time is not only possible, but under certain conditions inevitable, is clearly shown by the fact that, in writing a composition, it is necessary to attend simultaneously to at least four distinct elements—thought, language, spelling, and penmanship. To what extent incidental instruction may be carried can be discovered only by a study of results. As in some of our progressive schools the work in the formal branches has been tending for some years toward incidental instruction, opportunity is already offered for such study. In endeavoring to solve the problem by discussion, our educators are only wasting energy and losing valuable time.

The possibilities of incidental instruction are not limited to the formal studies, but extend to the content studies as well. In the latter, however, the ground covered in the different schools varies so markedly that we are unable to formulate tests which will lead to the comparative study of results. Investigation in the content studies will not be fruitful, therefore, until our goals are more definite and our notions clearer in regard to what results in these branches may be regarded as satisfactory. Moreover, as most of the time in the mechanical schools is devoted to the formal branches, incidental instruction in the content studies is a less urgent problem, at least for the present, than it is in the case of the formal ones.

When I speak of incidental instruction, I do not mean that satisfactory results might be secured if a branch were left to take care of itself. Incidental instruction, to be worthy the name, is not a *laissez-faire* system, but must be as carefully planned and as thoroughly and systematically conducted as if the subject were separately taught. If the teacher, for instance, should act on the theory that, in time, the pupil would learn to write neatly and legibly just because he writes, and accordingly would accept manuscript in any form in which it was presented, she would not be imparting incidental instruction, but would simply be neglecting penmanship. Incidental instruction in that branch would be represented by a consistent effort on the part of the teacher to secure neatness and legibility in everything that was written. Whether it is possible to carry this out, with little or no special drill in penmanship after the forms of the letters have been learned, is purely a matter of experience.

The second factor, mental fatigue, relates directly to the apportionment of time to individual branches. Experience proves that the results of teaching do not necessarily correspond to the amount of time devoted to a branch, or, in other words, that an increase in time beyond a certain point does not lead to a proportionate increase in results. In order that the labor may be fully rewarded, a lesson must close at the proper point, and work in that particular subject must not be resumed until the mind is again ready for it. In this problem, therefore, a double element is involved: first, the length of a recitation; and, secondly, the frequency of recitations in a given subject.

Closely related to the question of fatigue is that of the powers of mental assimilation. The number of ideas that can be digested in a given period is limited, and therefore in the apportionment of time the question of assimilation must be considered as well as that of fatigue. The two are, indeed, so closely connected that it is impossible to say where the dividing line should be drawn.

The arrangement of a school programme on a purely logical basis may involve, therefore, an enormous waste of time, for more reasons than one. In a recitation sixty minutes in length, twice as much ground can be covered, it is true, as in a recitation only thirty minutes in length; and, again, in four recitations a week in a given subject, twice as much ground can be covered as in two. It is not, however, the number of ideas presented to the child, but only those assimilated, that count. An individual who takes twice as much food as another does not on that account weigh twice as much. Indeed, one who loads his digestive organs with more food than can be absorbed by the system may not thrive so well as one who takes no more than he can digest, and thus saves those organs from a needless strain.

In the old-fashioned system, where the material for instruction is selected largely on the principle of filling out time, matters are poured into the mind without regard to its assimilative powers. Under this, the cramming method, facts may be remembered for a brief period; but, failing absorption, they are likely soon to fall into oblivion. By extraordinary pressure, enough ideas may be crowded into the mind to enable one to pass a good examination on an appointed day; but many of them will be forgotten so quickly that the results secured in an examination unexpectedly given only a few weeks later will not be nearly so favorable.

Again, the brain-cells might reach the saturation point for one class of ideas, but be still in perfect condition to absorb ideas of another kind, just as the amount of food of one kind that can be assimilated in a given time is no indication of how much can be assimilated if it is presented in proper variety. Thus, by carefully distributing the work, we might secure a full return in a great variety of subjects, while the same amount of time devoted to a few subjects might involve considerable waste.

That the results in a given subject are not determined by the amount of time devoted to it is clearly indicated by the fact that in Germany, although the classes are fully as large as they are here, the children in the first few years, with only three hours' daily instruction, appear to thrive on reading, penmanship, language, arithmetic, geography, nature-study, literature, religion, music, and drawing. Moreover, what is learned in the German schools is learned thoroughly.

When viewed from this standpoint, overburdening

the course does not mean teaching a large number of subjects, but introducing so many details in the subjects taught that certain brain-cells must necessarily labor beyond the point of fatigue and beyond the power of assimilation in order that the specified ground may be covered. What the length of a recitation period should be, and how much should be taught in a single lesson, can only be deduced from the results of years of teaching.

The number of recitations a week in a subject must be determined by the amount of time required for brain-cells that have been in active operation fully to recover their strength, and again be prepared for the process of assimilation. If they are set to work earlier, they labor under unfavorable conditions, and less will be accomplished in a given time than if the recuperation had been complete. And it is, in fact, an open question whether the results of five recitations per week in a given subject will be much greater than those secured by three. This point can only be determined by comparing the results obtained under a different apportionment of time. If, in particular instances, the results of instruction are not satisfactory, it is absolutely unsafe to draw the conclusion, as our conservative citizens are apt to do, that not enough time has been devoted to the subject. Before deciding, it would be wiser to learn whether the time set aside for the purpose had been properly employed. In recent years, fatigue, as an element in education, has received considerable attention; but the observations thus far made are only of suggestive value, and will not directly aid in settling the points here discussed.

The third factor presented in our problem, mental maturity, concerns the period of school life when the various branches of study may be most profitably begun. If subjects are presented too early, the process of assimilation will be slow and imperfect; while, if reserved for the proper period, possibly as much might be accomplished in a single year as otherwise in three or four years.

The subjects at present offering the most fruitful field for research of this nature are arithmetic and technical grammar. In regard to the former, the belief is growing that the time given to it in the first two or three years is in large part wasted, or, in other words, that if children should begin arithmetic in earnest at the age of nine or ten, they would soon overtake those who began at five or six. Whether or not this is true cannot be determined without positive data. The suggestion, however, is a valuable one. To solve the question, it is necessary to compare the results secured by pupils whose early education in arithmetic has been neglected, with the results obtained by those who have passed through a systematic course from the start.

In technical grammar a still more positive stand is taken. While in a few schools this subject is begun in the fourth year, and in most schools in the fifth, it is the opinion of many educators that all the time devoted to it below the eighth year, if not below the high school, is wasted. This again can be learned from results only.

To guard against waste in apportioning the time for instruction in individual branches constitutes only one part of the problem of educational economy. The other lies in the elimination of waste in the process of teaching; for, if the time is not profitably employed, the specified results will not be obtained within the allotted period.

In teaching, both science and art are brought into play. Science tells us, for example, that the greatest amount of labor is performed with a given amount of energy when the channels of least resistance are employed. This condition obtains in teaching when the ideas are introduced through channels that naturally appeal to the interests of the child. When the instruction is interesting, it will attract the attention and hold it during the recitation. If, on the other hand, the child is not interested, his mind will wander, and either he will not attend at all, or his attention will be incomplete; a part of the energy being wasted in overcoming the elements of distraction. As the time at the disposal of the teacher will not be fully utilized unless the mind of every child is at work, interest must be regarded as a fundamental factor in educational economy. To render instruction so interesting as to keep the mind of every child occupied will require intuition, judgment, and experience, as well as a knowledge of the theory of teaching.

A second point lies in securing a condition favorable to the assimilation of ideas. It is not enough to render instruction interesting. It is necessary as well to create a state of mental hunger—a desire for further knowledge when the recitation is over—so that the next lesson on the subject will be impatiently awaited. When the child is thus prepared for the acquisition of new ideas, and these ideas are presented at the proper moment, the process of assimilation will be most active. Therefore, although the powers of assimilation are limited, it yet lies within our reach to produce a mental attitude that will insure the greatest possible absorption of ideas. To carry this point successfully will tax the teacher's ingenuity to the utmost.

The third important factor for the elimination of waste in teaching lies in taking into account the individuality of the pupils. A teacher in charge of fifty children cannot, of course, be expected to consider all their peculiarities. Nevertheless, a great deal might be done if only this one point should receive attention, viz.: the differences in the degree of facility with which pupils grasp particular branches. Recitations properly adapted to one who readily comprehends new principles in a given subject cannot be followed with advantage by one who experiences great difficulty in learning them. Consequently, the teacher should avoid placing such pupils in the same group, or in some other way should exercise her ingenuity toward remedying the more glaring defects of this nature. The teacher will find an abundance of opportunity for the exercise of judgment by so instructing the class that, so far as possible, each child shall make even progress in the various branches of the grade.

To attain this end, a child who was quick in

arithmetic and slow in spelling, for example, might be excused more or less frequently from the regular recitations in the former, and be permitted to devote the time to the latter. Or, again, the brightest pupils might perform a valuable service in the way of individual instruction by helping those who are slow. To some extent a plan of mutual assistance might be instituted whereby children would help their comrades in one branch, and receive assistance from them in another. Teachers who have tried some such plan as this have found that children are often more successful than they themselves in clearing away the difficulties. One who has recently passed through certain difficulties appears better to understand where they lie than one who guesses at them from reminiscences or on purely theoretical grounds.

Finally, much waste is involved in keeping a child back because a low mark in one or two branches reduces his general average below the standard required for promotion. To compel a child to spend six months or a year in going over perfectly familiar ground in geography and arithmetic because he had failed in spelling and grammar, is, in truth, not wasting time, but stealing it; and it is worse than ordinary theft, because stolen time can never be replaced. Moreover, such an error of judgment in regard to promotion may rob the child of all ambition, kill his interest in intellectual work, and turn the entire current of his life.

Having pointed out the principles upon which an ideal system of education might be founded, I shall, in future chapters, discuss the data that I have collected through the practical application of these principles. As the problem is endless in its ramifications, I do not entertain the hope that my facts—which show the results of teaching in the case of a very large number of children—will be accepted as a positive solution. I shall, indeed, feel that my labor has been amply repaid if they should do no more than convince my readers that our elementary schools are conducted without regard to economy of effort, and that, so long as this condition prevails, the possibilities of elementary education will remain an unknown quantity.

V

THE FUTILITY OF THE SPELLING GRIND[1]

IN the opening chapters, I endeavored to prove that the first step toward placing elementary education on a scientific basis must necessarily lie in determining what results might be reasonably expected at the end of a given period of instruction. I there contended that if we had no definite notions in regard to what our teachers ought to accomplish, our ideas must be doubly vague as to how much time need be devoted to each branch. And, so long as this question remains unanswered, no well-founded opinion can be given concerning the possibility of broadening the course of study without detriment to the formal branches—the point around which the entire problem of educational reform revolves.

Believing that the most rational method of determining what our teachers might be expected to accomplish would lie in discovering what results the more successful ones had been able to obtain, I ventured to undertake the series of researches to which I have called attention, in the hope that it might serve as an initial step toward bringing this problem to a solution. And it is to the discussion of the data thus collected that this and the remaining chapters will be devoted.

[1] April, 1897.

The material to be submitted in this chapter and the next is intended to show what our teachers have accomplished in spelling, and what, therefore, may be reasonably demanded of our schools in that subject. The traditional standard in spelling is perfection; but this standard is unreasonable, and cannot be too soon abandoned. In view of the fact that in many cases the spelling faculty is weak, perfection could not be attained even if the number of words taught in an eight-year course should not exceed a thousand. And when we consider that the number of words in ordinary use is certainly not less than 15,000, including derivatives—and the derivatives are frequently difficult to spell—the absurdity of our demand becomes evident. Moreover, as some of our most scholarly people are deficient in spelling, and as, in this subject, some of the brightest pupils cannot keep pace with the dullest, our high-pitched sensibilities on the spelling question may be regarded as one of the mysteries of civilization. If these facts were more fully considered, we should undoubtedly feel more inclined to pardon an occasional mistake in spelling, and to refrain from abusing the schools for a weakness which, whatever might be done by our teachers, could not be overcome.

My researches in spelling were begun in February, 1895, and extended over a period of sixteen months. During this time three different tests were made; the number of children examined reaching nearly 33,000. In the present chapter, I shall merely state the results of these tests, with certain conclusions that I have drawn from them; deferring to the next the details concerning the methods of teaching, and the influences of certain modifying conditions, such as age, nationality, and environment, which were studied as closely as possible in order that the comparisons might be fairly drawn. The results of the various tests, which are shown side by side in the accompanying tables, will be fully explained.

My first test consisted of the following fifty words: furniture, chandelier, curtain, bureau, bedstead, ceiling, cellar, entrance, building, tailor, doctor, physician, musician, beggar, plumber, superintendent, engine, conductor, brakeman, baggage, machinery, Tuesday, Wednesday, Saturday, February, autumn, breakfast, chocolate, cabbage, dough, biscuit, celery, vegetable, scholar, geography, strait, Chicago, Mississippi, Missouri, Alleghanies, independent, confectionery, different, addition, division, arithmetic, decimal, lead, steel, pigeon. These words, together with a set of questions concerning the methods employed by the teachers, as well as particulars in regard to the pupils, were sent to school superintendents in various sections of the United States. Of these superintendents, some twenty responded; sending me, in total, the work of more than 16,000 children. Of the two tables presented with this chapter, the first shows the general average obtained in individual cities by grades, every class-room examined being represented in the figures; while the second shows the results in individual schools—the most characteristic among those examined having been selected for publication in this form. In the first table the results of two tests only are shown; while the second includes the results of the three. As it was thought inadvisable to publish the names of the localities from which the papers were received, the various cities have been represented by numbers, and the individual schools by letters.

On directing our attention to the results of the first test, we are startled by the enormous variations, when the extremes are considered—particularly in the fourth-year classes, where the averages range from 33 to 95.3 per cent. Such brilliant results as the latter might lead one to believe that the spelling problem had already been solved, and that nothing was needed to put all our teachers on the right path beyond a careful study of the methods employed where the highest marks had been secured, and then carrying the message to those whose results had been less favorable.

As the replies to my questions concerning the methods used by different teachers were not sufficiently clear to enable me to penetrate to the root of the matter, I decided to undertake a special tour for the purpose of obtaining more definite information from the teachers who had taken part in the test. During this tour, which extended over a period of two months, more than two hundred teachers were visited. Long before I had reached the end of my journey my fondest hopes had fled; for I had learned from many sources that the unusually favorable results in certain class-rooms did not represent the natural conditions, but were due to the peculiar manner in which the examinations had been conducted. As the tests had not been made under my personal supervision, I could not, of course, vouch for the figures; and, having found that under these circumstances experienced school people were unwilling to accept them, I was obliged to become resigned to the idea that most of my trouble had been for nothing.

An unfortunate feature of the first test was the fact that in many of the words careful enunciation would give the clue to the spelling. In such words, for example, as *tailor, doctor, different, independent,* the difficulty is entirely obviated by placing the accent on the last syllable. Under these circumstances, even the most conscientious teachers could not fail, unwittingly, to give their pupils some assistance, if their enunciation were habitually slow and distinct; while in those instances in which my test had been looked upon as an opportunity for an educational display—in which the imperfections of childhood were not to be shown—the teachers had been afforded the means of giving their pupils sufficient help, through exaggerated enunciation alone, to raise the class average very materially. I am confident, however, that, if any irregularities were practiced, they were committed without the knowledge of the superintendents, who, as a class, are well known to discountenance such acts and to do all in their power to stamp them out. That, moreover, in the vast majority of instances, the teachers were conscientious is proved by the numerous papers sent to me in which the results were unfavorable.

If I could safely have done so, I should have discarded the first test entirely rather than express these doubts. But to ignore this test might have submitted me to the charge of hiding results which did not substantiate my pedagogical theories; whereas, in truth, I had fully determined in advance to base my theories on the facts, whatever their nature might be. As the results of the second and third tests are placed side by side with those of the first, no danger can arise by presenting figures which, if shown by themselves, might be misleading.

In view of my doubts concerning the first test, I decided to undertake another, and personally to supervise the examinations. Moreover, by giving a second test I believed that I might be able to discover whether or not my fears had been well founded. In the latter the words were written in sentences; fifty test-words being employed in the fourth- and fifth-year classes, and seventy-five in the sixth, seventh, and eighth.[1] In preparing this test, special

[1] While *running* he *slipped.* I *listened* to his *queer speech,* but I did not *believe* any of it. The *weather* is *changeable.* His loud *whistling frightened* me. He is *always changing* his mind. His *chain* was *loose.* She was *baking* cake. I have a *piece* of it. Did you *receive* my letter? I heard the *laughter* in the *distance.* Why did you *choose* that *strange picture?* **Because* I *thought* I liked it. It is my *purpose* to *learn.* Did you *lose* your *almanac?* I gave it to my *neighbor.* *I was *writing* in my *language book.* Some children are not *careful enough.* Was it *necessary* to keep me *waiting* so long? Do not *disappoint* me so *often.* I have *covered* the

care was exercised to omit words whose pronunciation would tell the secret.

In the second test more than 13,000 children were examined under my personal direction; and the papers, although temporarily marked by the pupils, were finally corrected by my assistants. Although I could not be present in every room during the entire course of the examination, and although children cannot be prevented from copying, especially where the rooms are furnished with double seats and where the teachers have no control over their classes, I nevertheless believe that, for all practical purposes, the results of the second test demonstrate quite fairly what the children were able to do. In addition to those already mentioned, an indirect test in spelling was made in the form of compositions. The compositions represented the reproduction of a story specially prepared for the purpose.

mixture. He is *getting better.* *A *feather* is *light.* Do not *deceive* me. I am *driving* a new horse. *Is the *surface* of your desk *rough* or *smooth?* The children were *hopping.* This is *certainly* true. I was very *grateful* for my *elegant present.* If we have *patience* we shall *succeed.* He met with a *severe accident. Sometimes* children are not *sensible.* You had no *business* to *answer* him. You are not *sweeping properly.* Your reading shows *improvement.* The ride was very *fatiguing.* I am very *anxious* to hear the news. I *appreciate* your kindness, I *assure* you. I cannot *imagine* a more *peculiar character.* I *guarantee* the book will meet with your *approval. Intelligent* persons learn by *experience.* The peach is *delicious.* I *realize* the *importance* of the *occasion.* Every rule has *exceptions.* He is *thoroughly conscientious; therefore* I do trust him. The elevator is *ascending.* Too much *praise* is not *wholesome.*

The fourth- and fifth-year test ends with "This is *certainly* true." The higher test includes all the sentences except the four marked with an asterisk. The test-words are italicized.

This story, which was accompanied by a picture, was read to the pupils by the teacher. The compositions also, in a large number of schools, were prepared under my personal supervision, and in many others under the special supervision of persons whose conscientiousness could not be doubted. In those cases in which the papers were marked for spelling, I feel morally certain that the true results were shown.

The marks for the spelling in compositions, which may be found in Table No. 2, are based on the actual number of words written by the child, and represent the number of correctly spelled words per hundred. When the same word was misspelled more than once in an individual composition, one error only was counted. The average ages were computed from the returns of the first test. The details concerning this question, as well as the time devoted to spelling, will be more fully considered in the next chapter.

Of the three examinations, the first has been generally regarded as the least efficient in demonstrating the child's ability to spell, as such a test does not represent what he is able to do in ordinary writing. That this argument is worthy of some consideration, particularly in the case of the more immature children, is indicated by the fact that some of the fourth-year averages which on the first test were in the thirties, on the second advanced to the seventies. The second test appeared to meet with general approval, although a few teachers believed it too difficult for the sixth-year classes. As the test was purely comparative, however, this objection could not affect its validity. As to the comparative merits of the sentence- and the composition-tests, most teachers favor the latter, on the ground that the most rational test of the child's ability is one that shows his power to apply what he has learned. On the other hand, some have argued in favor of the sentence-test, believing that compositions do not include a sufficiently broad range of words to show the pupil's strength in all directions. If, however, an agreement might be secured to judge the spelling by the general written work, at least a temporary standard would be indicated by the results of my composition-test, which lead to certain definite conclusions.

In regard to the first test, I shall do no more here than direct attention to a few facts substantiating my statements concerning its validity. In the first place, it will be seen, by glancing over the averages in the last two columns of the second table, that the schools which towered above the others on the first test showed no marked superiority on the second. This is strikingly apparent in the case of School A, No. 9, which, on the first test, stood head and shoulders above the others, and, on the second, secured only eleventh place among the twenty-one on my list. The condition becomes doubly interesting when these marks are compared with those secured on both tests by School A, No. 7.

In order to allay my fear of harboring unwarranted suspicions in the case of the remarkable class average of 95.3, secured in the fourth grade of

Table No. 1.—General Averages for Cities.

City Number.	4th Grade. First Test. Average Age.	4th Grade. First Test. No. Papers Ex.	4th Grade. First Test. Average %.	4th Grade. Second Test. No. Papers Ex.	4th Grade. Second Test. Average %.	5th Grade. First Test. Average Age.	5th Grade. First Test. No. Papers Ex.	5th Grade. First Test. Average %.	5th Grade. Second Test. No. Papers Ex.	5th Grade. Second Test. Average %.	6th Grade. First Test. Average Age.	6th Grade. First Test. No. Papers Ex.	6th Grade. First Test. Average %.	6th Grade. Second Test. No. Papers Ex.	6th Grade. Second Test. Average %.	7th Grade. First Test. Average Age.	7th Grade. First Test. No. Papers Ex.	7th Grade. First Test. Average %.	7th Grade. Second Test. No. Papers Ex.	7th Grade. Second Test. Average %.	8th Grade. First Test. Average Age.	8th Grade. First Test. No. Papers Ex.	8th Grade. First Test. Average %.	8th Grade. Second Test. No. Papers Ex.	8th Grade. Second Test. Average %.	City Number.
1	11.4	205	70.8	114	66.7	12.4	171	78.1	120	78.1	13.2	131	86.9	91	74.9	14.3	123	88	74	77.6	15	86	93.6	87	84.6	1
2	10.9	183	51.9	.....	.....	11.6	194	67.6	.....	.....	12.9	218	75.4	.....	.....	13.8	187	84.3	.....	.....	14.6	187	89	.....	.....	2
3	12.2	147	56.1	.....	.....	13.3	78	66.9	.....	.....	13.8	58	76.6	.....	.....	14.8	40	81	.....	.....	16	23	82	.....	.....	3
4	12.7	174	50	.....	.....	12.4	190	64.3	.....	.....	13.3	123	71.3	.....	.....	14	120	82.7	.....	.....	14.9	153	85.5	.....	.....	4
5	10.7	94	62.9	.....	.....	11.8	145	69.5	.....	.....	13.7	172	79.8	.....	.....	13.5	147	84	.....	.....	14.3	81	85.7	.....	.....	5
6	11.6	132	61.8	.....	.....	12.3	140	70	.....	.....	13	104	81.5	.....	.....	14.5	91	79.5	.....	.....	15.4	66	81	.....	.....	6
7	11.1	479	41.3	304	63.9	11.9	436	58.6	319	75.3	12.9	553	67.9	432	69.4	13.7	574	78	283	76.5	14.8	376	82.1	409	82.8	7
8	11.6	166	46.7	.....	.....	12.2	137	59.4	.....	.....	13.2	120	81.3	.....	.....	14.6	123	79.6	.....	.....	15	86	86	.....	.....	8
9	11.4	132	79.6	345	67.9	12.6	239	83	312	76	13.7	382	86.5	251	73.2	14.8	232	89.6	229	82.8	.....	.....	.....	.....	.....	9
10	11.1	146	45.4	191	65.4	12.4	165	65	200	73.8	13.6	91	69.8	194	67.4	14.2	87	74.9	86	81	15.2	98	78.5	100	83.3	10
11	11.2	213	53.6	.....	.....	12.5	132	66.6	.....	.....	13.1	197	79	.....	.....	14.5	140	83.7	.....	.....	15	50	90.9	.....	.....	11
12	.....	.....	.....	466	57.7	.....	.....	.....	362	73.4	.....	.....	.....	237	75.9	.....	.....	.....	89	84.6	.....	.....	.....	154	90.6	12
13	12	280	56.5	.....	.....	13.1	296	66	.....	.....	14	137	75	.....	.....	14.6	165	79.8	.....	.....	15.9	59	85.1	.....	.....	13
14	11.2	236	57.5	.....	.....	12	240	65.3	.....	.....	12.7	179	71.3	.....	.....	14.3	206	77	.....	.....	14.5	188	82.2	.....	.....	14
15	.....	120	54.1	389	69.3	.....	87	68.2	525	77	.....	64	73.7	401	70	.....	78	85.6	262	79.8	.....	73	89.6	211	86.1	15
16	11	142	47.6	173	64.7	12.2	150	62.2	189	75.1	13.2	150	68.7	107	63.8	14	110	76.4	175	72.7	15.3	123	77.7	127	81.8	16
17	11.6	129	50.2	.....	.....	12.4	138	64	.....	.....	12.6	121	76.1	.....	.....	14	100	78.2	.....	.....	15.3	81	84.9	.....	.....	17
18	11.6	194	56.5	.....	.....	12.7	172	71.9	.....	.....	13.5	162	81.9	.....	.....	14.4	36	87	.....	.....	.....	.....	.....	.....	.....	18
19	11.1	227	55.3	146	59.1	12.7	326	67.3	209	71.2	13.8	327	73.8	164	67.7	14.6	298	79	172	78.3	15.7	231	86.1	133	83.5	19
20	11.8	264	48.7	.....	.....	12.7	286	68.4	.....	.....	13.2	269	72	.....	.....	14.3	254	82.8	.....	.....	15.6	144	86	.....	.....	20
21	11.1	157	51.5	.....	.....	12.2	97	59.5	.....	.....	12.9	104	73.3	.....	.....	14	73	79.6	.....	.....	14.9	57	82.3	.....	.....	21
General Averages.	.....	3820	53.5	2128	64.2	.....	3819	64.3	2236	75.1	.....	3662	75.6	1877	70.4	.....	3184	81	1370	78.8	.....	2162	84.2	1221	84.4	General Averages.

School A, No. 9, I compared the papers of the individual pupils who had taken part in the first test with those presented by the same pupils on the second. Most of these pupils, in the meantime, had been promoted to the fifth grade. Of course, if their papers had again shown the same degree of perfection, it would have been but fair to conclude that the figures at first secured were reliable, and that we had simply discovered a remarkable group of children. The second examination proved, however, that these children had not been born in Wonderland, but that they were of the very same stamp as other children had proved to be. In fact, the average made on the second test by those who had received 95.3 on the first was only 73, or exactly the same as that made by the pupils of School A, No. 7, who on the first test obtained not more than 41.

In Schools E and H, No. 15, the figures are reliable, as the words were dictated by myself. Again, in City 18, the examinations were made in my presence, the words being dictated by the teachers. In no instance in which the tests were made under my supervision—the words being pronounced by either the teacher or myself—was the class average for the fourth year, in boys' or mixed schools, higher than 59 per cent. I desire to say, in passing, that the results in the girls' schools were higher than those in the boys' and mixed schools. In the accompanying tables the girls' schools have been omitted; otherwise the comparison would have been misleading. They will be considered separately.

Leaving the first test and directing our attention to the others, we are confronted by a number of interesting phenomena, almost equally manifest in both. The most striking of these are: First, that in the vast majority of instances the results are very close when the averages for entire buildings are compared. In fifteen of the twenty-one schools on my list, the averages on the second test, as the table shows, run from 73.3 to 77.9. Second, while the results in the lower grades of different schools show considerable variation, those in the eighth-year classes, which represent the end of the school course, are remarkably even. In twelve of the seventeen eighth-year grades, the averages are from 84 to 88, the A and B classes being taken together. And in fifteen of a total of twenty sets of eighth-grade compositions examined for spelling, the variations were only three-tenths of 1 per cent, the results lying between 99.1 and 99.4, the A's and B's being taken as one. These facts are doubly remarkable when we consider that the twenty-one schools not only represent institutions in many sections of the country, but that they are samples of schools conducted under all conceivable conditions. For example, No. 7 is a Western city of moderate size, while No. 15 is a large city in the East. Again, most of the children attending School A, No. 7, are of American parentage, and their home surroundings are particularly favorable; while the children attending School B, No. 7, represent the foreign laboring element. Further, from a pedagogical standpoint, all varieties of schools are included; some of them belonging to the most mechanical, while others are among the most progressive, in our country.

If the best results had been secured in the mechanical and the poorest in the progressive schools, the question would arise whether the small additional return would warrant the latter in placing additional pressure on spelling at the expense of other subjects. But even this question does not arise; for it did not happen that the results in most cases were best in mechanical schools. Indeed, in both the mechanical and the progressive schools the results were variable; so that while, in some instances, the higher figures were secured by the former, in others they were obtained by the latter; and the same is true of the lower figures. For example, School B, No. 11, in which the best average (79.4) was obtained, belongs to a very progressive system; while School A, No. 12, which made only 73.9, belongs to one of our most mechanical systems. And it is a peculiar incident that, in both these cities, the results in the only other school examined are exactly reversed, although the environment is about the same.

Further, just as it is impossible by the results to distinguish the mechanical from the progressive schools, so it is impossible to distinguish the schools attended by the children of cultured parents from those representing the foreign laboring element; the results from this standpoint also varying equally. Consequently, so far as spelling is concerned, the influence of environment appears to be insignificant.

The second point to which I have referred,

namely, the small variation in the eighth-year results—regardless of how much time had been devoted to spelling, or what methods had been employed, or under what home influences the children had been reared—is also well worthy of consideration. And it is no less striking that the same level was reached in the end, regardless of what had been accomplished in the lower grades, a fact which becomes obvious on comparing the results in the eighth-year classes with the average obtained by the entire school. In the composition test, where the results in fifteen of the twenty sets of eighth-year papers were within three-tenths of each other, this fact is still more clearly demonstrated. To make a further study of eighth-year results a few variations in the tests were tried, but no modifications were found. For example, in a special test of twenty-five very simple words, I examined four eighth-year classes representing three different cities. The extremes did not vary more than two points; the results being respectively 92.0, 93.2, 93.6, and 94.4. In one school, the compositions were written from the picture alone, so that the pupils were absolutely free in the selection of the story and the choice of words. The average was 99.3.

Do not these results indicate that, in learning to spell, maturity is the leading factor, while method plays only a subordinate part? And, if the superiority of the old-fashioned spelling grind cannot be demonstrated, is it not our duty to save the child from this grind? Moreover, as the results prove that, beyond a certain minimum, the compensation for time devoted to spelling is scarcely, if at all, appreciable, have we not here discovered an element of waste, which, if eliminated, would open the way to an equal enrichment of the course of study without detriment to the formal branches?

It might still be argued that while pressure could be omitted in the case of pupils who were likely to complete the grammar-school course, it would nevertheless be needed for those who cannot attend school longer than four or five years. But, in view of my results, this argument is equally controvertible. For, in the first place, while the fourth and fifth grades, individually considered, show considerable variation, we find many instances in which a low fourth-year average is followed by a high fifth, and *vice versa;* so that when the two grades are averaged together, the results for the different schools are very close. Again, while the differences in the fourth year are marked, the results do not speak in favor of mechanical primary schools. On the contrary, the poorest fourth-grade results—Schools A and B, No. 12—were obtained by the pupils of primary departments as mechanical as any to be found; while, on the other hand, among those who did best were included some of our most delightful primary schools, such as School A, No. 7, and School B, No. 11. That no dogmatic statements on this point can be made on either side, however, is proved by the fact that a contrary statement would be equally true; for in some of the mechanical schools the fourth-grade averages were high, while in some of the progressive schools they were comparatively low.

In the majority of instances, the results of the first test, also, were confined within narrow limits; for, in twelve out of eighteen cities—Nos. 1 and 9 being excluded—the averages ranged from 70.6 to 74.8, the number of correctly spelled words thus lying between 35 and 37. On the second test, the general averages in seven cities out of nine ranged from 73.5 to 76.8. The smallest variations, however, were found in the results of the composition-test, where, in spite of the great variation in the character of the institutions, the extreme difference in ten schools out of eleven was only five-tenths of 1 per cent—98.2 to 98.7.

Finally, as in most localities the general results were nearly equal—those secured under the same system of instruction varying as much as those obtained under different systems—it is clear that the remedy does not lie either in a change of method or in an increase of time. And this conclusion accords with the fact that the dissatisfaction with spelling is as great in communities where this subject constitutes a special feature as in those where spelling plays only a subordinate part in the schools.

Whether or not the spelling in a particular locality is actually below the average can only be learned by comparing the results of an examination conducted on the same basis in many localities. By examining children in any one city, on a set of arbitrarily selected words, the question cannot be solved, because the results in other places, on the same list of words, would remain an unknown quantity. A common standard is offered, however, by a composition-test such as I have undertaken. And when a test of this nature shows results similar to those presented in this article, interested citizens may rest assured that the spelling in their own schools is no worse than it is in those of most other localities.

VI

THE FUTILITY OF THE SPELLING GRIND—II [1]

In the preceding chapter I showed what our teachers had been able to accomplish in spelling, and, consequently, what standards in this subject we were justified in establishing. Thus far, the feasibility of establishing definite standards has been denied, on the ground that the influence of instruction was so profoundly modified by conditions inherent in the pupils that the results obtained in one class-room would not necessarily indicate what we had a right to expect in another. In the present chapter, however, I shall endeavor to prove, by an analysis of the factors involved, that, so far as spelling is concerned, the results are not dependent on conditions over which the teacher has no control, but that, whether satisfactory or unsatisfactory, the causes may be found on the side of instruction. When my analysis is completed, I shall present an outline of what my investigations have led me to regard as the most rational plan of treating the subject.

In presenting my data, I shall first direct attention individually to the factors brought into play by the pupils, viz., age, nationality, heredity, and

[1] June, 1897.

environment, and show how the mysteries are dissipated when the first ray of light is thrown upon them. The elements involved in instruction will then be considered in the same manner.

If the ability to spell were influenced by age, the results, naturally, would be in favor of the older pupils. That the averages received by these were not higher than those obtained by the younger ones, however, is proved by the figures presented in Table No. 1. These figures show, on the contrary, that in the majority of instances the results were in favor of the younger pupils. This may be accounted for by the fact that the younger children in a class are frequently the brighter and the more mature, having overtaken the older pupils by reason of these characteristics. Moreover, that the best spellers are to be found, as a rule, among the brightest pupils, is shown by Table No. 2, which indicates the influence of intellect on spelling. As the task of computing the results by ages, intellect, and so on, from the papers of individual children was found to be very laborious, not all the papers received were utilized for this purpose.

As in the preceding chapter, the cities are indicated in the tables by numbers, and the individual schools by letters. The first test, it will be recalled, consisted of a column of fifty words, and the second, of sentences; fifty test-words being employed in the fourth and fifth, and seventy-five in the sixth, seventh, and eighth-year classes. The third test, spelling in compositions, will not be considered here. In Table No. 2, which shows the influence of intellect on spell-

TABLE No. 1.

	City.	FOURTH YEAR. Age.	No. of Pupils.	Genl. Average.	FIFTH YEAR. Age.	No. of Pupils.	Genl. Average.	SIXTH YEAR. Age.	No. of Pupils.	Genl. Average.	SEVENTH YEAR. Age.	No. of Pupils.	Genl. Average.	EIGHTH YEAR. Age.	No. of Pupils.	Genl. Average.
COLUMN-TEST.	1	9-11	131	72.5	9-12	107	78.	9-13	72	85.9	9-14	88	88.5	12-14	24	94.4
	"	12-15	78	67.4	13-17	69	75.9	14-17	56	84.9	15-17	38	86.6	15-18	60	93.5
	2	9-12	167	51.5	10-12	136	71.	11-13	137	77.	11-13	82	86.5	12-14	76	90.9
	"	13-16	16	55.1	13-15	57	59.9	14-17	63	74.1	14-16	105	83.1	15-19	111	86.6
	11	9-11	111	56.1	10-12	61	70.1	10-13	112	75.1	11-14	77	83.2	13-15	37	90.5
	"	12-15	104	48.1	13-16	91	63.5	14-17	74	78.3	15-18	63	84.	16-18	13	91.7
SENTENCE-TEST.	1	9-11	72	69.5	10-12	56	81.6	12-13	22	79.9	12-14	43	76.7	12-14	35	86.9
	"	12-15	39	59.1	13-15	38	78.8	14-16	10	68.3	15-17	21	77.8	15-17	52	84.9
	*7	8-10	47	68.9	10-12	56	81.4	12-13	22	79.2	12-14	43	76.6	12-14	35	87.2
	"	11-13	27	59.	13-15	38	78.9	14-16	10	68.3	15-17	21	77.8	15-17	52	84.8
	†9	9-11	55	70.2	10-12	38	75.5	11-13	38	73.1	12-14	44	86.2			
	"	12-15	51	64.7	13-15	45	76.2	14-16	55	74.7	15-17	32	86.5			

* School A. † School B.

TABLE No. 2.

No. of Cities.	Grade.	No. of Classes.	No. Pupils Intellect 1.	Average.	No. Pupils Intellect 2.	Average.	No. Pupils Intellect 3.	Average.	No. Pupils Intellect 4.	Average.
3	4	16	112	78.7	169	70.5	152	58.8	54	52.1
3	5	16	117	86.	239	77.7	166	71.1	59	61.6
3	6	23	164	88.7	263	84.3	182	78.	69	73.7
3	7	19	116	93.4	216	88.3	155	77.5	59	79.2
2	8	8	56	94.	99	89.3	97	87.8	20	81.5

TABLE No. 3.

	GRADE.	No. of Cities.	No. of Classes.	No. of Pupils.	General Average.	Children of Foreign Parentage.	Average.	No. of Children hearing Foreign Language at home	Average.	Children of Unskilled Laborers.	Average.
COLUMN-TEST.	Fourth..........	21	119	3700	53.5	1051	52.	815	52.	670	53.2
	Fifth..........	21	126	3560	64.3	1126	66.3	814	65.1	619	64.2
	Sixth..........	21	122	3594	75.6	1032	74.9	790	74.1	584	74.3
	Seventh.........	21	109	3107	81.	914	81.6	621	80.9	361	79.
	Eighth..........	21	71	2088	84.2	608	85.3	345	85.9	204	82.
SENTENCE-TEST.	Fourth..........	4	27	821	64.7	155	65.2	159	64.9	129	62.5
	Fifth..........	4	29	829	76.	153	77.4	157	76.7	129	74.5
	Sixth..........	4	22	778	69.7	185	69.6	165	70.3	119	70.4
	Seventh.........	4	18	566	78.8	81	82.5	52	81.5	55	76.8
	Eighth..........	4	19	528	83.1	72	83.2	64	83.2	76	85.

ing, "Intellect 1" indicates the brightest, and "Intellect 4," the dullest pupils. The difference in favor of the brightest pupils, when compared with the dullest, is very striking. The lesson to be learned from Table 2 is that an unusually high or low class-average may now and then be accounted for by an exceptionally bright or dull set of pupils. Occasionally, therefore, the teacher may be allowed to plead "dull pupils" as an excuse for poor results. While this might offer a loophole for an incompetent teacher, the danger of being misled by such a plea is not great, because, in most instances, the teacher's statement can be verified by reference to the principal. Teachers habitually cursed with dull pupils cannot be placed too soon on the retired list. If the results throughout a building should be unsatisfactory, to plead "dull pupils" would, of course, be ridiculous.

Next, a comparison of the results obtained by children representing the foreign element with those secured by the American element (Table No. 3) shows that the influence of nationality on spelling is nil. Indeed, the percentages, if not identical, are slightly in favor of the foreign element. These figures, computed from the papers of pupils attending schools of all varieties, are substantiated by the fact already mentioned; viz., that the results in schools attended almost entirely by children of foreigners were fully as good as those in schools where most of the pupils were from American homes. Moreover, in spelling, nationality furnishes a very broad clue to heredity. And as the excellent spelling so frequently found among the children of foreigners cannot be regarded as the perpetuation of a family trait, the influence of heredity on spelling must also be put down as immaterial.

In Table No. 3, the influence of environment is also shown; the results obtained by children of unskilled laborers, whose home surroundings are presumably unfavorable, being compared with results obtained by all classes of children examined. And here again, strange as it may seem, the percentages were practically equal; thus showing that home environment exerts, apparently, as little influence on spelling as the other factors that I have discussed.

As the facts I have presented would indicate that the results of instruction in spelling were not materially modified by conditions over which the teacher had no control, it is evident that the causes of success and failure must be sought among the elements brought into play by the teacher. The most important of these are: (1) the amount of time devoted to spelling; (2) the methods of teaching the subject; (3) the selection of words; and (4) the personal equation of the teacher. These points will now be individually considered.

Concerning the amount of time devoted to spelling, I need only repeat what was mentioned in the preceding chapter, namely, that an increase of time beyond a certain maximum is not rewarded by better results, or, in other words, that all the time beyond this maximum is simply thrown away. This, in my opinion, was conclusively proved by the table presented in that chapter, which showed that the results obtained by forty or fifty minutes' daily instruction were not better than those obtained where not more than ten or fifteen minutes had been devoted to the subject. As the time element is the central point around which the possibility of enriching the course revolves, my researches would have been amply repaid if they had led to nothing beyond this discovery.

Those who regard as incredible my statement concerning the time element in spelling may possibly find some food for reflection in Chapter III. Again, conviction may be carried by the facts presented in a letter from Dr. Eucken, Professor of Philosophy in the University of Jena. Professor Eucken writes as follows:

JENA, April 19, 1897.

MY DEAR DOCTOR:

I have read your articles in *The Forum* with great interest; and I am pleased that you are laboring with so much energy toward the exclusion of useless matters from the course, so that attention may be centred on the essentials. The results presented in your last article, "The Futility of the Spelling Grind," are also very interesting, and cannot fail to lead to serious reflection.

That instruction, particularly in the lower grades, is in need of simplification, we have had occasion to experience with our own children. It appeared to us that, for the little the children actually acquired in the public schools, they were obliged to spend far too much time in the schoolroom. We therefore organized a small private class (3 to 5 children) for the purpose of covering the work of the lower grades. The children received from 5 to 8 hours' instruction per week. The results were perfectly satisfactory. The requirements were met excellently, so that the children were enabled immediately to enter the next higher grade.

No doubt the number of pupils played an important part

in the achievement; but the success must certainly be largely attributed to the better methods employed in our little private school.

I therefore wish you all possible success in your endeavors. Obviously, in America, they are duly recognized and appreciated.

Very respectfully yours,

DR. J. M. RICE. R. EUCKEN.

Next, concerning the influence of methods, a very comprehensive study was made, through personal interviews with some two hundred teachers whose pupils had taken part in my tests. These teachers were questioned, to the minutest details, in regard to the course they had pursued. As the table showing a summary of these interviews side by side with the results was found too complicated for publication, I shall be able to present only the deductions to be drawn therefrom.

In brief, these deductions may be summarized in the statement that there is no direct relation between methods and results. In other words, the results varied as much under the same as they did under different methods of instruction.

For example, among the points that have given rise to endless discussion is that concerning the value of oral spelling; some believing it to be vital, while others claim that it is actually detrimental. My tests showed that, while in some of the schools where a special feature had been made of oral spelling the results were favorable, in others they were unfavorable. And the same conditions were shown where oral spelling had been abandoned. Secondly, much discussion has arisen as to whether, in written spelling, the words of the lesson should be placed in columns or in sentences. But the claim of superiority in favor of sentence over column spelling was by no means corroborated, the results of the sentence method varying just as much as those of the column method.

In addition to questions on the fundamental elements, an inquiry was made concerning the details relating to these methods; such as the mode of dividing words into syllables, both in oral and written spelling, the different ways in which misspelled words were made up by the pupils, the frequency of reviews, and so on. But no direct relation between devices and results could be traced. A very careful study was made as to whether there is any foundation for the theory that when children learn to read by the phonic method they fall into the habit of spelling phonetically, and therefore become poor spellers. The analysis showed that some of the best results had been obtained where the phonic method had been employed; that, in fact, the phonic method had long formed a feature in the cities where the highest averages were made. Another theory, that the best spelling is produced in schools where the most general reading is done, also proved unfounded. Nor did the schools where the most time was devoted to written language make the best showing.

A device known as the sight or flash method has also found its way into some of our schools. This method, in brief, is as follows: A word is written on the board by the teacher, who permits the pupils to glance at it for a moment. The word is then erased, and the pupils are called upon to reproduce it on the board from memory. In this way, one word after another is written until the lesson is completed. Some who have used this method look upon it as a panacea: others have no confidence in it whatever. Judging by my results, the claims in its favor are not warranted. On the contrary, in some of the schools where it had been faithfully tried, the results were particularly discouraging.

The facts here presented will, in my opinion, admit of one conclusion only; viz., that the results are not determined by the methods employed, but by the ability of those who use them. In other words, the first place must be given to the personal equation of the teacher, while methods and devices play only a subordinate part.

It seems to me, therefore, that the evils now ascribed to uncontrollable circumstances should be attributed in large part to a lack on the part of the teacher of those qualifications which are essential to success. Consequently, when reasonable demands are not met within a reasonable time limit, we are justified in inferring that the fault lies with the teacher and not with the pupils. An instructive experience I once encountered will serve to illustrate this point. On leaving a class-room in which I had heard a few recitations, I complimented the teacher on the intelligence of her pupils. She replied: "You must not give me credit for that. *These children are Russians; and one can do anything with Russians.*" It so happened that on the next day, I visited a class-room, in which the children were exceptionally dull. On this occasion the teacher remarked: "You must not blame me for their stupidity. *My pupils are Russians; and one cannot do anything with Russians.*"

Finally, I shall call attention to an important factor, on the side of instruction, whose influence, though manifest, is not affected by the spirit of the teacher. I refer to the selection of words for the spelling course. It is in this element only that I can find an explanation of the most puzzling feature shown in the tables accompanying the preceding article, namely, that classes which received exceptionally low averages on the column test did just as well as others on the sentence and composition tests. That these poor results cannot be attributed to lack of experience in writing words in columns is proved by the fact that, in most of the schools where they were secured, column spelling had formed a regular feature in instruction. Nor can they be accounted for by the fact, previously mentioned, that the exceptionally high percentages were not trustworthy; for the results to which I now refer were far below those obtained in some instances where the words were dictated by myself. I believe, therefore, that the lack of success on this particular test was due to the fact that it contained certain classes of words on which these pupils had not been drilled; although, with few exceptions, the words employed were very common ones.

A careful analysis showed that in most instances where the low averages on the column test were obtained, the spelling-book had been abandoned;

although where it had been set aside the results were not always low. In many such cases, the words are selected entirely from the other school-books—reader, geography, history, arithmetic, science, and so on—when opportunity for using them in school work arises. Words not directly needed are liable to be neglected, however common they may be. Thus, in selecting words for the needs of the schoolroom, rather than of life, the danger arises of giving precedence to technical and unusual words, while the common ones play a subordinate part only.

It is claimed in favor of this method of selection that it is the more natural one. In my opinion, however, no method of teaching can be more unnatural; for, when the words are thus selected, the pedagogical principle—from the easy to the difficult—is disregarded, and systematic progress abandoned. Moreover, from a practical standpoint, the method is a most wasteful one, because much of the time which should be devoted to practical spelling is spent in studying words seldom used outside the schoolroom. When the need for such words arises in life, resort may be had to the dictionary. If the dictionary must be more or less frequently employed, in spite of instruction in spelling, it is safer to run our chances with the unusual words than with those in constant use. The danger of leading children into bad habits if we permit them to misspell words in their written work could be obviated without completely perverting instruction in spelling. It would be necessary simply to tell the pupils how to spell the uncommon and technical words, or to place them on the board, when occasion required. Thus, children might be led incidentally to learn how to spell the rarer words, while the spelling period proper might be spent on practical work.

The absurdities incident to the so-called "natural method" were shown very clearly during one of my visits to a fifth-year class, when the pupils, who had studied the pine, were about to write a composition on the subject. In preparation, the spelling-lesson of the day consisted of the following words: *Exogen*, *erect*, *cylindrical*, *coniferal*, *irregular*, *indestructible*, *pins*, *resinous*, and *whorls*. First, as for systematic progress in spelling—from the easy to the difficult—a more absurd combination could be scarcely devised. And, secondly, from the practical point of view, such words as *exogen*, *coniferal*, *whorls*, are entirely out of place—at least until perfection in common words has been reached. And that drill in common words was still sorely needed in this instance was shown by the results obtained by the pupils on some of the simple words in my sentence test; the forty-four papers submitted showing errors as follows: *running* 9, *slipped* 27, *believe* 17, *changeable* 30, *baking* 7, *piece* 11, *careful* 12, *waiting* 9, *getting* 9, *driving* 11, and *hopping* 17. In the grade representing the latter half of the fourth school-year, containing pupils soon to be promoted into the class just spoken of, the results in forty papers on words in my column test showed the following errors: *bureau* and *chocolate* 39, 36, *Wednesday* 34, *dough* 31, *autumn* 27, *cabbage pigeon* 38, *biscuit*, *celery*, *vegetable* 37, *February*

24, *bedstead, beggar, steel* 23, *tailor* 22. Are we justified in such cases as these in spending our time on unusual words?

Having presented my data, it will now be in place to say a few words concerning the course in spelling which I have been led to regard as the most rational and fruitful. First, as to oral and written, column and sentence, spelling, I shall say only this, that the wise teacher will acquaint herself with as many methods and devices as possible, and change from one to the other, in order to relieve the tedium and to meet the needs of individual children. Before all, she will beware of running off at a tangent with any particular method, because none yet discovered has proved a panacea.

Secondly, under no circumstances should more than fifteen minutes daily be devoted to the subject. Whatever benefit the pupils receive from their instruction in spelling will be obtained within this period.

Thirdly, I should recommend that the words be carefully graded, not only in regard to orthographical difficulties, but in accordance with the vocabulary of the child as well. In this way, the course in spelling might become as systematic as in other subjects.

Fourthly, precedence should be given to common words, while technical and unusual words should be taught incidentally. By excluding words of the latter classes, the course would be materially abridged, and the chances of producing good practical spellers proportionately increased.

Fifthly, the course should be further abridged by excluding words that contain no catch, *i.e.*, words which naturally spell themselves. My researches on this point would indicate that more than half the common words belong to this category and consequently need not be studied. The ideal ground to be covered in spelling would be represented, therefore, by a carefully graded list of the common words most liable to be misspelled. The number of words in this list, according to my estimate, would be between six and seven thousand.

When the words have been selected, the next step will lie in a systematic treatment of the difficulties. And here again the course is open to simplification, by separating the words that may be learned collectively from those which must be mastered individually.

The words that can be acquired collectively are those to which rules of spelling apply. While, in some instances, the exceptions are so numerous as to rob the rules of their value, a few of them, nevertheless, are very reliable, at least for all practical purposes. And, as these few rules govern thousands of words, it would be much less burdensome to master them than to memorize such words individually. Among these rules, two are particularly comprehensive, and should be taught, year after year, until applied automatically. They are: first, the rule referring to the doubling of the consonant, as in *run-running;* and, secondly, the rule concerning the dropping of the final *e*, as in *bake-baking*. That so many children, even in the highest grammar grade, should spell *lose* with two *o's* does not necessarily throw discredit on the teacher; but that a child who has attended school four years or more should write "While runing he sliped," or "She was bakeing cake," is as unpardonable as if he were unable to add 2 and 2. And yet out of 252 pupils in the fourth school-year, whose papers were examined with reference to this point, *running* was misspelled by 94, *slipped* by 126, and *baking* by 69.

That little advantage is now taken of rules is indicated by the fact that, broadly speaking, as many errors were made on words governed by rules as on those to which they did not apply. The comparison is shown in the following table, which is based on the sentence test:

TABLE No. 4

No. of Schools.	Grade.	No. of Pupils.	General Average.	Results on words under the rule.	Results on words not under rule.
3	4	252	66.4	60.9	69.0
3	5	232	76.4	72.6	78.2
3	6	311	71.0	73.2	70.2
3	7	191	80.9	81.9	80.6
2	8	62	86.3	91.4	85.4

In the fourth and fifth year classes, it will be seen that the results were in favor of words not under the rule. In the sixth year classes, however, the scale began to turn.

The words that must be studied individually are those in which no clue is given, either by sounds or rules. The best to be done with such words, until our spelling is reformed, is to bring them to the notice of the child, and trust to chance for the results. The simple reform of dropping the silent letter in the last syllable of such words as *beggar, driver, doctor, mantel, bundle, metal,* would enable us to strike no less than 15 per cent of the words from the described list. Again, in the long vowel sounds the difficulties are endless; the same sound being represented in so many different ways that it is a marvel to be able to master them at all. To illustrate: *blue, to, too, two, who, shoe, you, ewe; lieu, view, new (knew); no (know), sew, beau, toe, owe, oh, dough, goat.* Again, the choice between *ee* and *ea,* as in *feed, read,* is extremely puzzling. What a boon to our children it would be to rid spelling of such peculiarities as these!

The difficulties in English spelling were most vividly demonstrated by the numerous ways in which the younger children endeavored to get at some of the words. In a fourth year class of forty pupils, for example, the word *physician* was misspelled in forty different ways, *chandelier* in 32, *machinery* in 27, *bureau* and *chocolate* in 23, *vegetable* in 19, *furniture* in 18, *biscuit* in 17, *Wednesday* in 15, *celery* and *pigeon* in 14, *baggage* in 13, *February* and *cabbage* in 11, *dough* in 9. Some of the combinations were as follows:

For *physician: fasition, fesition, fisition, fusition, fazition, fisision, facision, fizeshon, fazishon, fusashon, physichan, phyzision, physicion, phacicion, physision, phisishon, phasichian, phisishon, vasition, vecrtion, fasision, fosishen, fursishon, fushistion, feshishon, phisican, fusison, fesision, phsishen, fazuishen, phosion, fusion, fysion, fazshen, fishon, phasian, phacion, fegtion, phyasishen, phsam;* for *chocolate: chocalate, choclate, choclet, chocklet, chocklate, chockolit, chocklod, chokolat, chokelate, choklat, chalkolet, chaclote, chaclate, chalket, cholet, cholate, choalate, chalcolate, choctlet, choaklate, choclelot, chouilet, cacklet;* for *bureau: buro, burow, buroe, buerow, burreau, burro, burou, buero, beauro, beaurow, beaurew, beuro, beuroe, berro, berow, berrow, biro, beiro, brewro, bewer, beroueo, broe, berrobe;* for *vegetable: vegitable, vegitabels, vegatable, vegtable, vegtible, vegtibale, vegeatabel, vegitble, vegitbul, vegatobol, vegitale, vetable, vegeable, vegubale, veguable, vegatabe, vegitalb, vegtful, vestuble;* for *furniture: furnature, furnishture, funeture, funiture, furnutor, furnisher, furnachure, furnichure, fruniture, furiture, furnerchur, ferichure, furicher, furichur, furuner, ferichrue, furercure.*

Finally, I would suggest a separate list of those puzzling small words, which, though constantly used in writing, are yet so frequently misspelled. Among these may be mentioned *to, too, there, their, hear, here, any, many, much, such, which, those, whose,* and *does.* In all such a list need not include more than 150 or 200 words. As these words cannot be too often brought to the notice of the child, the drill should be begun as early as possible and continued throughout the entire course. Even in the highest grammar grade, a considerable number of pupils will write *dose* for *does*, *who's* for *whose*, *there* for *their*, *to* for *too*, etc. The sentence, "Too much food is harmful," was given to very many children East and West; and in the sixth year classes from 40 to 75 per cent of the pupils began the sentence with "To."

Although a liberal admixture of methods and a judicious selection of words would be of material assistance, nothing can take the place of that personal power which distinguishes the successful from the unsuccessful teacher. Consequently, our efforts should be primarily directed toward supplying our schools with competent teachers. As the number required precludes the possibility of limiting the selection to those who are born for the profession, our only course lies in developing the requisite powers, as well as we can, where they are naturally weak. To this end, I believe that no means can be more effective than to prescribe a definite task, to be completed in a given time, and to make the tenure of office depend on the ability to meet the demand. If my proposition should consider the results alone, then of course it would be fraught with the danger of leading us back to the era of endless mechanical drill; but so long as the time limit is a *sine qua non*, this danger is entirely averted.

VII

A TEST IN ARITHMETIC [1]

In the present and the following two chapters, I shall present the facts secured by a test in arithmetic, and I shall concentrate attention chiefly upon the two fundamental questions by which teachers are confronted whenever a subject is incorporated in the school programme:

(1) What results shall be accomplished? and (2) How much time shall be devoted to the branch?

Intimately associated with these questions is a third, namely: Why do some schools succeed in securing satisfactory results with a reasonable appropriation of time, while others cannot get reasonable results in spite of an inordinate provision of time? This question introduces a problem which is much more involved than the others. Although no previous attempts have been made to discover which schools have really met with success in the teaching of a subject, under a given time allotment, and which have not, the facts are not difficult to secure. They must, however, be determined before any sustained forward movement in pedagogy becomes possible; otherwise our basis of pedagogical reasoning is liable to be false. Every practical educator who

[1] October-December, 1902.

endeavors to influence other members of the profession must necessarily base his pedagogical utterances on the assumption that the teaching in his own schools has been successful. In the absence of facts his word must be taken on faith, while the facts may prove that our adviser is wrong and that success has been met where it has been least expected.

As I have said, to get at the facts in regard to the results of instruction is a comparatively simple matter. Their explanation, however, is by no means easy. The educator of to-day finds no difficulty in explaining results, because he starts out with psychological theories and determines the results of his methods by a process of reasoning. He states, for example, that if such and such methods are used, such and such results must follow; but the results which he explains by the methods are the products of his own imagination. As long as he feels assured that certain results *must* follow his methods, why should he waste time in seeing that they do? When, however, we come into possession of real facts, we find that they differ widely from imaginary ones, and that theories which are a perfect fit to imaginary facts may not in any way fit the actual ones. In my researches I look for the genuine facts; and if the facts I find look queer and fail to bear out some of our long-cherished theories, do not let us blame the facts, but let us reconstruct our theories.

The test in arithmetic on which this article will be based was taken in the early part of the present year (1902). I made a similar test some six years ago, soon after I had completed the one in spelling; but my editorial duties at the time prevented me from following up the investigations in a satisfactory manner, and I therefore did not publish the results. In my recent test the examinations were made—in each instance during my presence—in eighteen school buildings, representing seven cities. In all, about 6,000 children were examined. While the number of pupils tested was, therefore, not nearly so large as in the case of my examinations in spelling, the investigation, nevertheless, sufficed to show the general conditions equally well from several points of view.

The test itself consisted of eight examples. In the first two schools ten were given, but some curtailment seemed advisable. As in my earlier tests, so in the recent one, the examinations were given to the pupils of the fourth, fifth, sixth, seventh, and eighth school years, representing, generally speaking, the grammar grades. They were not given below the fourth year, because the principal point, after all, is to see what the children are able to do on leaving school, and very few leave before the end of the fourth year.

In preparing my questions I endeavored to arrange them in a way that would suit the individual grades of all schools, regardless of the methods or systems employed. From this standpoint I was successful, excepting that in a very few instances two of the examples were beyond the scope of the pupils in the first half of the fourth year, because they had not yet learned to multiply or divide with figures above twelve, and in the first half of the seventh year, where the classes had not yet had much practice in percentage. These points were carefully noted; but when the papers were marked it was found that the effect upon the entire school average would not in any case exceed two per cent. I wish to add, furthermore, that for the purpose of studying the growth of mental power from year to year, some of the problems were carried through several grades. Thus, of the eight questions for the fourth grade, five were repeated in the fifth, and three in the sixth, etc. Moreover, this repetition will enable us to see not only, for instance, how the results in the fifth and sixth grades, in regard to certain problems, compare with those of the fourth in the same school, but also how the results in the fourth grade of some schools compare in these examples with those of the fifth and sixth grades of others, etc. The problems for all the grades may be seen on pages 122, 123, 124, and 125.

A discussion of the results will now be in order. In my investigation of the spelling problem, the striking feature, in regard to the results, was the fact that the differences were small, and particularly so in the upper grades. In arithmetic, on the other hand, the differences were large all along the line, and much greater in the seventh and eighth year classes than in the earlier ones. In the seventh year, the class averages ranged from 8.9 per cent to 81.1, and in the eighth year, from 11.3 to 91.7. The averages for schools taken as a whole varied between 25 and 80 per cent; and the extremes did not represent isolated cases, but were merely the ends of a graduated scale. In some schools low marks in two or three grades were offset by high marks in the others, producing a fair percentage. In others, fair results, grade for grade, produced a fair school average. In another class of cases the marks were good throughout, and in still another low throughout.

Table I gives two averages for each grade as well as for each school as a whole. Thus, the school at the top shows averages of 80.3 and 83.5, and the one at the bottom, 25.2 and 31.8. The first represents the percentage of answers which were absolutely correct; the second shows what per cent of the problems were correct in principle, *i.e.*, the average that would have been received if no mechanical errors had been made. The difference represents the percentage of mechanical errors, which, I believe, in most instances, makes a surprisingly small appearance.[1] For the sake of uniformity, I shall use the figures of the first column as the basis of comparison, although, in view of the very small differences, the

[1] The method of computing the mechanical errors requires an explanation. In examining the papers, only those examples that had been correctly worked in principle were considered; the others were marked wrong, and no further account was taken of them. Consequently, the percentage of mechanical errors is represented by the errors of that nature in the problems that had received credit for the principle. Thus, the figures for the school at the top show, in round numbers, that out of every 83 examples correct in principle, 3 contained mechanical errors. The latter are therefore represented by the fraction $3/83$, which is equivalent to 3.6 per cent. In the case of the school at the bottom, the fraction is $6/31$, equivalent to 19.3 per cent. In the table the percentages are slightly different, because the decimals also were considered.

same remarks would have applied to the other column as well.

If, for the purpose of analysis, the schools be divided into three classes—good, fair, and poor—the question of distribution becomes interesting, because, in nearly all cases, the different schools of an individual city will be found to belong to one and the same class. Thus, every one of the four schools of City I made a very good average; the three schools of City VI and the three of City VII show, without exception, very poor results; and of the four buildings in City IV, three did fairly and one did poorly. The only marked exception is to be found in City III, one of whose schools heads the table, while the other did only fairly well.

As for City I, by comparing the percentages for each grade with the general average for that grade, *i.e.*, the averages for all schools examined taken collectively, it will be seen that in one only of the nineteen classes represented did the grade average fall below the general average, the results in all other instances being above. On the other hand, of the fifteen classes of City VI, one only crossed the general average for the grade, while the results in the others were far below; and of the fifteen classes of City VII, one only touched the general average, several of the others being very far below. City IV saved itself from a low classification through favorable results, for the most part, in the fourth and fifth years.

The single school in City II secured high marks in the fourth, fifth, and sixth years, but did poorly in the seventh and eighth; while the single school in City V just met the general average in the fifth and eighth years, but fell far below it in the others.

After this review of the figures, it will be appropriate to ask why the results in the schools of City I were so much more favorable than those in the schools of Cities VI and VII. The layman would be disposed to reply at once that arithmetic had been better taught in the schools of the former city than in those of the latter. On the other hand, many thoughtful educators would not accept this offhand statement, but would claim that so many factors come into play in the education of the child that it is impossible to tell to what extent results are due to the teaching and in how far they are modified by other causes.

It is evident, therefore, that in seeking an explanation for the differences in the results, two factors must be taken into consideration: first, the influence of the teaching; and, secondly, the resistance against that influence due to circumstances over which the teacher has no direct control. It may be argued that if the resistance be great, superior teaching may be followed by poor results, and, on the other hand, that if the resistance be small, inferior teaching may be rewarded by excellent results. But it must also be admitted that if the resistance be equal, good results in one case and poor results in another must be credited to a difference in the quality of the teaching.

That the amount of resistance offered by non-pedagogical influences is to-day unknown does not by any means indicate that it must forever remain unknown. On the contrary, the problem of modifying conditions is not at all difficult to solve if we will but look it squarely in the face, divide it into its component parts, and study each factor independently. Analysis of the problem will show that the essential elements of which it is composed do not exceed three in number: (1) The home environment of the pupils; (2) the size of the classes; and (3) the average age of the children.

Now there is no mystery in regard to any of these points. All the facts may be readily ascertained and their value determined without great difficulty. As to the home environment of the pupils, the neighborhood in which a school is placed will be frequently sufficient to tell the story. Some schools are attended, for the most part, by children whose parents are considerably above the average in culture and material possessions; in others, the majority of the pupils are from homes where the parents themselves are less cultured and less favorably situated financially, but are fully as solicitous for the welfare of their children; while some schools are situated in the slums, where the pupils have the poorest of supervision at home. In regard to the size of the classes and the average age of the pupils, the facts are, of course, at hand.

A study of the figures in the table from these several standpoints will show conclusively that the influence of all these factors has been very much exaggerated, and, therefore, that the cause of unfavorable results must be sought, largely, at least,

TABLE I

	School.	4		5		6		7		8		SCHOOL AVERAGE.			Minutes daily.	When taken.
		Result.	Principle.	Result.	Principle.	Result.	Principle.	Result.	Principle.	Result.	Principle.	Result.	Principle.	Per cent. of mechanical errors.		
City III	1	68.4	76.7	79.5	82 5	79 3	80.3	81.1	82.8	91.7	93.9	80.0	83.1	3.7	53	A.M.
City I	1	72.7	81.4	84 7	88.8	80 4	81.5	64.2	67.2	80.9	82.8	76.6	80.3	4.6	60	A.M.
City I	2	....	....	80 3	87.1	80 9	83.4	43.5	50.9	72.7	79.1	69.3	75.1	7.7	45	A.M.
City I	3	54.5	66.0	74,7	78.3	72.2	74.0	63.5	66.2	74.5	76.6	67.8	72.2	6.1	45	A.M.
City I	4	60.0	78.3	70.8	79.3	69.6	72.2	54.6	57.8	66.5	69.1	64.3	70 3	8.5	45	P.M.
City II	1	81.3	87.7	78.2	85.6	71.2	75.3	33.6	35.7	36.8	40.0	60.2	64.8	7.1	60	P.M.
City III	2	70.1	79.9	53.6	60.0	43.7	45.0	53.9	56.7	51.1	53.1	54.5	58.9	7.4	60	P.M.
City IV	1	70.5	76.4	73.2	77.7	58.9	60.4	31.2	34.1	41.6	43.5	55.1	58.4	5.6	60	A.M.
City IV	2	62.9	72.8	70.5	76.8	59.8	63.1	....	....	22.5	22.5	53.9	58.8	8.3	..	P.M.
City IV	3	59.8	72.7	65.3	73.5	54.9	58.1	35.2	38.6	43.5	45.0	51.5	57.6	10.5	60	A.M.
City IV	4	53.5	62.2	53.5	65.7	42.3	45,1	16.1	19.2	48.7	48.7	42.8	48.2	11.2	..	P.M.
City V	1	38.5	46.3	67.0	71.0	44 1	48.7	29.2	32.5	51.1	58.3	45.9	51.3	10.5	40	P.M.
City VI	1	28.1	31.7	38.1	44.2	68 3	71.3	33.5	36.6	26.9	30.7	39.0	42.9	9.0	33	A.M.
City VI	2	41.6	51.9	45.3	52.1	46.1	49 5	19.5	24.2	30.2	40.6	36.5	43.6	16.2	30	P.M.
City VI	3	36.8	54.2	55.0	62.8	34.5	36 4	30.5	35.1	23.3	24.1	36.0	42 5	15.2	48	P.M.
City VII	1	59.3	69.3	53.7	63.1	35.2	37.7	29.1	32.5	25.1	27.2	40.5	45.9	11.7	42	A.M.
City VII	2	47.4	55.2	65.4	71.4	35.2	38.7	15.0	16.4	19.6	21.2	36.5	40 6	10.1	45	P.M.
City VII	3	41.1	58.0	37.5	44.5	27.6	33.7	8.9	10.1	11.3	11.3	25.8	31.5	19.6	45+	P.M.
General average	...	59.5	69.9	69.4	75.5	60.7	63.2	39.4	42.5	49.4	51.9	55.7	60 6	8.1		
Per cent of mechanical errors	....	....	14.8	....	8.1	....	3.9	....	7.3	....	4.8					
Number of pupils examined	....	....	1,422	....	1,593	....	1,285	....	974	....	689	Total, 5,963.				

on the pedagogical side. I shall not attempt, in the present paper, to enter into the discussion of the pedagogical aspect of the problem, but shall try to throw some light on that phase in the next chapter. Here I shall merely endeavor to show that in suggesting a standard as to time and results, the complicating conditions have all been considered.

If the part that is played by the home environment should be as important as it is generally supposed to be, we should, of course, expect to find that the schools represented in the upper part of the table had been attended by children from cultured homes, while those in the lower part had been attended by those whose home environment was very poor. However, if a line should be drawn across the middle of the table, and the schools above it compared with those below, such a condition would not be found. Indeed, careful inspection would show that the odds were certainly not in favor of the "aristocratic" districts. Of the eighteen schools, three in particular are representative of the latter, and the best of these secured the tenth place, while the others ranked eleventh and sixteenth, respectively. The school that ranked seventh was distinctively a school of the slums. That is to say, the school laboring under the poorest conditions in respect to home environment obtained a better standing than any one of the so-called aristocratic schools. The building which stands fifth is representative of conditions just a shade better than those of the slums. And when I add that, from the standpoint of environment, the schools of City I did not average a single degree better than those of Cities VI and VII, I have said enough to show that the poor results secured in the latter cities cannot be condoned on the ground of unfavorable environment. Thus, as in spelling, so in arithmetic, this mountain, upon close inspection, dwindles down to the size of a molehill.

Equally surprising, if indeed not more incredible, may appear the statement that no allowance whatever is to be made for the size of the class in judging the results of my test. I shall not enter into the details in regard to this point, but will dismiss it with the remark that the number of pupils per class was larger in the highest six schools than it was in the schools of City VI, and that the classes were exceptionally small in the school that stands at the lower end.

The relation between the age of the pupil and his arithmetical power is a question which has been very widely discussed. Some educators have taken the stand that there is not much object in laying stress on arithmetic in the early years; that arithmetical power increases naturally with age; and that any deficiency that may be manifest in the lower grades will be readily compensated for by the rapidity with which the children progress when they enter the higher ones. The belief has, therefore, become quite general that there is a direct relation between age and results; and for this reason many teachers might be inclined to attribute the variations in results to differences in the ages of the pupils, grade for grade, in the different schools.

As in other pedagogical problems, so in this, facts

prove how little dependence is to be placed on *a priori* reasoning. That there is a regular improvement in arithmetic as the child at school advances in years is perfectly true; and this point is very clearly shown by the fact that, with very few exceptions, the class averages on the repeated problems improve from grade to grade. But this in itself does not give us the information we are seeking. In the first place, the figures alone do not tell us to what extent the improvement was due to age, in how far it was the result of practice, or what part had been played by instruction. Besides, it should not be forgotten that the problem with which we are now dealing is not a qualitative, but a quantitative, one. That children improve as they advance from grade to grade may be taken for granted. It is the rate of progress with which we are concerned.

That the differences in results in the schools examined were not due to differences in age may be readily shown by eliminating the age factor entirely, which may be done by taking the age of the pupils instead of the grade as the basis of comparison. For this purpose Table II has been prepared. That table is based on the results obtained upon problems that were carried through three grades. The fourth, fifth, and sixth year papers contained three problems in common, and this is true also of the papers for the sixth, seventh, and eighth grades.[1] The table shows, first, the results obtained in the fourth, fifth, and sixth grades of the highest six schools as

[1]See the first three problems for the sixth and eighth years cn pages 123 and 125.

compared with the lowest six, taken collectively, upon the repeated problems; secondly, those obtained upon the repeated problems in the sixth, seventh, and eighth grades of the highest five schools as compared with the lowest six; and, thirdly, the average ages of the pupils in the grades and schools stated.

I did not have an opportunity to obtain the ages of the pupils of all the schools considered in Table II. However, in computing the average ages the majority of these schools were represented, and the complete returns could not have changed the figures more than a month or two one way or the other. If the comparisons had been made between the schools where the ages had all been obtained, the showing would have been practically the same as in the table. Moreover, in arithmetic, the differences in the results are so very marked all along the line that microscopic distinctions are in no way called for.

TABLE II.

	4		5		6	
	Average age.	Per cent.	Average age.	Per cent.	Average age.	Per cent.
Six highest schools...	11.9	62.8	12.6	84.3	13.4	96.3
Six lowest schools....	11.0	29.0	12.0	49.8	13.4	61.4
	6		7		8	
Five highest schools..	13.4	49.5	14.1	71.9	14.11	90.4
Six lowest schools....	13.4	11.0	13.11	29.0	14.5	38.0

A glance at the ages will show that the average age of the pupils of the schools that showed the best results was about five months higher than that of the pupils of the schools that did poorest. For the fourth grade the difference was nine months, and for the fifth and eighth grades, six months. In the sixth and seventh grades, however, the ages were practically the same. But the factor of age may be completely eliminated by comparing the results of a given grade of the successful schools with those of a higher grade of the unsuccessful ones. Thus, in the fourth grade of the successful schools the average was 62.8, as against 49.8 in the fifth year, and 61.4 in the sixth year of the unsuccessful ones. Consequently, in this instance, the results in the unsuccessful schools did not equal those of the successful ones until the pupils were nineteen months older and had had the advantage of two years' additional instruction and practice.

Similar comparisons in regard to the higher grades show even a greater disparity, as the eighth year pupils of the unsuccessful schools did not even catch up to those of the sixth year of the successful ones. In the case of the sixth and seventh year classes, where the ages were practically alike, the full class averages may be compared. For the sixth year they were 75.6 as against 41.1; and for the seventh year 61.4 as against 22.8. These facts certainly constitute a striking blow at the theory of those who believe that arithmetic is a matter of natural evolution.

One other point here calls for consideration. The

idea is generally accepted that an examination in arithmetic given in the morning will show much more favorable results than one given in the afternoon; and it might, therefore, be supposed that the schools that did best had been examined in the morning, and *vice versa.*

When the table is analyzed from this standpoint the indications appear to favor the theory; but the quantitative aspect has certainly been exaggerated. Looking at the facts, we find that the first four schools in the order of merit had been examined in the morning. However, in the school which stands fifth, the examination was given in the afternoon, and the average was 64 per cent, or only 3 per cent lower than that of the school next preceding, and 5 per cent lower than the school that ranked third. The point of particular interest is the fact that the school, by being examined in the afternoon, did not lose its classification. The first three schools of City I were examined in the morning and did well. The fourth school of that city was examined in the afternoon and also did well.

In City VI, School 1 was examined in the morning, and did 3 per cent better than those examined in the afternoon, obtaining an average of 39 as against 36; and School 1, City VII, by being examined in the morning, secured an average of 40 per cent. In a word, Schools 2 and 3, City VI, were examined in the afternoon and did poorly; School 1 of the same city was examined in the morning and also did poorly. And the same remarks apply to City VII. Thus, while there seems to be some advantage in an examination given in the morning, the figures appear to leave no doubt that a school that can do well in the morning can also do well in the afternoon, and, conversely, that a school that does poorly in the afternoon will also do poorly in the morning. I have heard it stated that the difference between a morning and an afternoon examination will probably reach 20 per cent. If so, what would have been the result if School 1, City VI, and School 1, City VII, had been examined in the afternoon?

Now, taking all the facts into consideration, which of the schools examined may be said to have made a satisfactory showing? Personally, I believe the demand is not placed too high when the line dividing the satisfactory from the unsatisfactory schools is drawn across the table under School 4, City I, the last of the buildings making creditable averages in all the grades. In the school next in order the results were more than satisfactory in the fourth, fifth, and sixth grades, but unsatisfactory in the seventh and eighth. All the other schools showed too many weak spots to be passed as satisfactory.

The general average for all schools examined was, in round numbers, 55 per cent, made up as follows: 60 per cent for the fourth year, 70 per cent for the fifth, 60 per cent for the sixth, 40 per cent for the seventh, and 50 per cent for the eighth. In view of what the satisfactory schools have shown, it seems to me that 60 per cent for the fourth grade, 70 per cent for the fifth, and 60 per cent for the sixth are reasonable expectations. However, 40 per cent for the seventh grade and 50 per cent for the eighth are too low, as these figures are not at all representative of what the successful schools have been able to accomplish, but result from the fact that, in the majority of instances, the seventh and eighth grades were lamentably weak. As the average for the seventh grade of the five successful schools was 61.4, and that for the eighth grade 77.2, I think that less than 50 per cent for the seventh year and 60 per cent for the eighth should not be regarded as satisfactory. This would raise the general average from 55 to 60. But a school average of 60 per cent or more should not be looked upon as satisfactory unless the grade averages were met in four cases out of the five. A provision for failure in one grade is reasonable, because there may have been particular causes of failure in an individual class. The children may have been exceptionally dull, or the class may have been in the hands of a substitute, etc. But, in my opinion, failure in more than one grade denotes a weakness which calls for a remedy. The above figures apply to a test taken at, or any time after, the middle of the year.

In suggesting a standard, it is, of course, understood that the figures mentioned in the last paragraph would only be applicable to an examination whose degree of difficulty was the same as my own. Teachers desirous of knowing how their pupils compared with those of other schools could try the questions as I have given them; or, if they feared that the publication of the problems had diminished the value of the test, they might change the figures without altering the degree of difficulty. However, in due course of time there ought to be no difficulty in establishing standards in arithmetic with mathematical precision. This may be quite readily done by selecting types of examples and determining by research what percentage ought to be obtained on each of them by the class for which they are intended. When this point has been reached, a standard will also have been fixed for a combination of examples of various degrees of difficulty.

In the present chapter I shall not endeavor to suggest a standard in regard to the mechanical side of arithmetic, as a discussion of the details of that phase of the question would carry us too far. I merely wish to call attention to a fact which may appear strange to the majority of teachers, namely, that, from the standpoint of results, the mechanical side of arithmetic has shown itself to be very closely related to the thought side. In other words, the schools that showed the best thinking also made the smallest number of mechanical errors. Indeed, when we compare the first six schools in the table with the last six, we find the school average 69.7 as against 35.8, or double, while the percentage of mechanical errors is 6.1 as against 13, or half. Therefore, broadly speaking, a stipulated demand in regard to the thought side of arithmetic includes, indirectly, a demand in relation to the mechanical side.

A glance at the general average of mechanical errors shows a marked improvement from the fourth grade to the sixth, the percentages being 14.8, 8.1, and 3.9, respectively. Thus, in round numbers, only half as many errors were made in the fifth year as in the fourth, and only half as many in the sixth year as in the fifth. That the improvement in mechanical arithmetic should be so decided from grade to grade may be readily explained by the fact that simple computation appeals altogether to the memory, which fixes the various combinations of numbers more and more firmly as the result of endless repetition.

The figures show that the number of mechanical errors was larger in the seventh and eighth years than in the sixth. This, however, does not indicate retrogression, but is due to the fact that the basis of comparison was not the same. In the upper two grades the mistakes were made principally in the placing of the decimal point—an element that did not come into play, to any considerable extent, in the lower grades. The seventh and eighth year classes, however, are again compared on practically the same basis, and, as before, the difference is marked in favor of the higher grade.

Let us now see what can be learned from Table I as to the relation between the time devoted to arithmetic and the results. We shall then be in a position to form an estimate regarding the amount of time that should be allowed with a view to the accomplishment of satisfactory results.

A glance at the figures will tell us at once that there is no direct relation between time and results; that special pressure does not necessarily lead to success, and, conversely, that lack of pressure does not necessarily mean failure.

In the first place, it is interesting to note that the amount of time devoted to arithmetic in the school that obtained the lowest average, 25 per cent, was practically the same as it was in the one where the highest average, 80 per cent, was obtained. In the former the regular time for arithmetic in all grades was forty-five minutes a day, but some additional time was given. In the latter the time varied in the different classes, but averaged fifty-three minutes daily. This shows an extreme variation in results under the same appropriation of time.

Looking again toward the bottom of the list, we find three schools with an average of 36 per cent. In one of these, insufficient pressure might be suggested as a reason for the unsatisfactory results, only thirty minutes daily having been devoted to arithmetic. The second school, however, gave forty-eight, while the third gave forty-five. This certainly seems to indicate that a radical defect in the quality of instruction cannot be offset by an increase in quantity.

From these few facts two important deductions may be made: First, that the unsatisfactory results cannot be accounted for on the ground of insufficient instruction; and, secondly, that the schools showing the favorable results cannot be accused of having made a fetich of arithmetic. These statements are further justified by the fact that the four schools of City I, which, on the whole, stood highest, gave practically the same amount of time to arithmetic as the three schools of City VII, which stood lowest.

Now, bearing in mind the standard suggested in regard to the results, what should be set down as a reasonable time allowance?

A glance at Table I will show us that out of the eighteen schools examined, five only succeeded in obtaining satisfactory results, and that the time devoted to arithmetic in these schools varied from forty-five to sixty minutes a day. Taking the schools in the order of merit, the time allotment was fifty-three, sixty, and forty-five minutes. That the highest two schools had given fifty-three and sixty, respectively, does not indicate that they could not have met the demand if the time had been limited to forty-five. Indeed, the results secured in the school at the top show such a very large margin above the demand that a reduction of eight minutes per day could not have sufficed to shatter the structure, and a similar assumption may be made in the case of the school standing next. As the conditions under which the five successful schools labored were not in any way exceptional, I think it is perfectly reasonable to say that the results ought to be satisfactory if the time be limited to forty-five minutes a day. All the schools that succeeded proved their ability to do the work in forty-five minutes, and most of the schools that failed proved their inability to succeed in spite of even a larger appropriation of time.

While the facts appear to indicate that forty-five minutes will suffice, they do not show that that amount of time is actually required to accomplish satisfactory results. It is true that out of the five schools giving less than forty-five minutes, the results were unsatisfactory in four. Of the latter, one school gave forty-two minutes and obtained an average of 40 per cent, an average so far below the margin that an additional three minutes could not possibly have saved the day. Similar remarks are applicable to the school where a time allotment of forty minutes was followed by an average of 45 per cent. In City VI, the schools that gave thirty and thirty-three minutes, respectively, obtained averages of only 36 and 39 per cent; but in the other school of that locality, where the time was forty-eight minutes, the results were not any better. It is clear, therefore, that the failure in these four unsuccessful schools was not due simply to the fact that the time was less than forty-five minutes.

In spelling, it was not difficult to draw conclusions as to the limit of useful instruction—the point where attention and effort cease and beyond which additional pressure is not rewarded by additional return. A large proportion of the schools having reduced the time, it was possible to institute comparisons on a broad scale between the results obtained where much time had been devoted to spelling and those secured where but little time had been given to it; and it was seen that the schools devoting forty minutes a day to spelling did not do any better than the schools where but ten or fifteen minutes had been given to the subject. This proved that there was nothing to be gained by continuing the instruction beyond fifteen minutes a day. In arithmetic, on the other hand, the basis of comparison from the standpoint of time is not nearly so wide, as it is still the custom in the vast majority of the schools to devote at least forty-five minutes daily to the subject. For the present let us accept forty-five minutes as a reasonable time allowance for arithmetic; but let us reduce the allowance if we should succeed in finding a reasonable number of schools showing satisfactory results with less instruction.

The discussion in the preceding pages has tended to show that arithmetic presents certain difficulties which are quite readily overcome in some schools, while seemingly insurmountable in others. As the teachers, taken all in all, were apparently as conscientious and as well trained in the schools that failed as in those that succeeded, it is reasonable to suppose that the principal cause of failure has been a matter of misdirected effort. But whatever the trouble may be, it is evident that its nature must be clearly understood before remedial measures can be intelligently discussed. Therefore, the next step in our researches must lie in endeavoring to discover the source of the trouble; and I shall present some facts regarding this point in the next chapter.

FOURTH YEAR.

1. A man bought a lot of land for $1,743, and built upon it a house costing $5,482. He sold them both for $10,000. How much money did he make?

2. If a boy pays $2.83 for a hundred papers, and sells them at four cents apiece, how much money does he make?

3. If there were 4,839 class-rooms in New York City, and 47 children in each class-room, how many children would there be in the New York schools?

4. A man bought a farm for $16,575, paying $85 an acre. How many acres were there in the farm?

5. What will 24 quarts of cream cost at $1.20 a gallon?

6. A lady bought 4 pounds of coffee at 27 cents a pound, 16 pounds of flour at 4 cents a pound, 15 pounds of sugar at 6 cents a pound, and a basket of peaches for 95 cents. She handed the storekeeper a $10 note. How much change did she receive?

7. I have $9,786. How much more must I have in order to be able to pay for a farm worth $17,225?

8. If I buy 8 dozen pencils at 37 cents a dozen, and sell them at 5 cents apiece, how much money do I make?

FIFTH YEAR.

1. A man bought a lot of land for $1,743, and built upon it a house costing $5,482. He sold them both together for $10,000. How much did he make?

2. If a boy pays $2.83 for a hundred papers, and sells them at four cents apiece, how much does he make?

3. What will 24 quarts of cream cost at $1.20 a gallon?

4. If I buy 8 dozen pencils at 37 cents a dozen, and sell them at 5 cents apiece, how much money do I make?

5. A flour merchant bought 1,437 barrels of flour at $7 a barrel. He sold 900 of these barrels at $9 a barrel, and the remainder at $6 a barrel. How much did he make?

6. How many feet long is a telegraph wire extending from New York to New Haven, a distance of 74 miles? There are 5,280 feet in a mile.

7. A merchant bought 15 pieces of cloth, each containing 62 yards. He sold 234 yards. How many dress patterns of 12 yards each did he have left?

8. Frank had $3.08. He spent $\frac{1}{4}$ of it for a cap, $\frac{1}{7}$ of it for a ball, and with the remainder bought a book. How much did the book cost?

SIXTH YEAR.

1. If a boy pays $2.83 for a hundred papers, and sells them at 4 cents apiece, how much does he make?

2. What will 24 quarts of cream cost at $1.20 a gallon?

3. If I buy 8 dozen pencils at 37 cents a dozen, and sell them at 5 cents apiece, how much do I make?

4. A flour merchant bought 1,437 barrels of flour at $7 a barrel. He sold 900 of these barrels at $9 a barrel, and the remainder at $6 a barrel. How much did he make?

5. If a train runs 31⅔ miles an hour, how long will it take the train to run from Buffalo to Omaha, a distance of 1,045 miles?

6. If a map 10 inches wide and 16 inches long is made on a scale of 50 miles to the inch, what is the area in square miles that the map represents?

7. The salt water which was obtained from the bottom of a mine of rock salt contained 0.08 of its weight of pure salt. What weight of salt water was it necessary to evaporate in order to obtain 3,896 pounds of salt?

8. A gentleman gave away 1/7 of the books in his library, lent 1/6 of the remainder, and sold 1/5 of what was left. He then had 420 books remaining. How many had he at first?

SEVENTH YEAR.

1. If a map 10 inches wide and 16 inches long is made on a scale of 50 miles to the inch, what is the area in square miles that the map represents?

2. The salt water which was obtained from the bottom of a mine of rock salt contained 0.08 of its weight of pure salt. What weight of salt water was it necessary to evaporate in order to obtain 3,896 pounds of salt?

3. A gentleman gave away 1/7 of the books in his library, lent 1/6 of the remainder, and sold 1/5 of what was left. He then had 420 books remaining. How many had he at first?

4. A farmer's wife bought 2.75 yards of table linen at $0.87 a yard and 16 yards of flannel at $0.55 a yard. She paid in butter at $0.27 a pound. How many pounds of butter was she obliged to give?

5. If coffee sold at 33 cents a pound gives a profit of 10 per cent, what per cent of profit would there be if it were sold at 36 cents a pound?

6. Sold steel at $27.60 a ton, with a profit of 15 per cent, and a total profit of $184.50. What quantity was sold?

7. If a woman can weave 1 inch of rag carpet a yard wide in 4 minutes, how many hours will she be obliged to work in order to weave the carpet for a room 24 feet long and 24 feet wide? No deduction is to be made for waste.

8. A fruit dealer bought 300 apples at the rate of 5 for a cent, and 300 at 4 for a cent. He sold them all at the rate of 8 for 5 cents. What per cent did he gain on investment?

EIGHTH YEAR.

1. If a map 10 inches wide and 16 inches long is made on a scale of 50 miles to the inch, what is the area in square miles that the map represents?

2. The salt water which was obtained from the bottom of a mine of rock salt contained 0.08 of its weight of pure salt. What weight of salt water was it necessary to evaporate in order to obtain 3,896 pounds of salt?

3. A gentleman gave away 1/7 of the books in his library, lent 1/6 of the remainder, and sold 1/5 of what was left. He then had 420 books remaining. How many had he at first?

4. A man sold 50 horses at $126.00 each. On one-half of them he made 20 per cent, and on the other half he lost 10 per cent. How much did he gain?

5. Sold steel at $27.60 a ton, with a profit of 15 per cent, and a total profit of $184.50. What quantity was sold?

6. A fruit dealer bought 300 apples at the rate of 5 for a cent, and 300 at 4 for a cent. He sold them all at the rate of 8 for 5 cents. What per cent did he gain on his investment?

7. The insurance on 2/3 of the value of a hotel and furniture cost $420.00. The rate being 70 cents on $100.00, what was the value of the property?

8. Gunpowder is composed of nitre 15 parts, charcoal 3 parts, and sulphur 2 parts. How much of each in 360 pounds of powder?

VIII

CAUSES OF SUCCESS AND FAILURE IN ARITHMETIC [1]

In the preceding chapter I presented the results of my test in arithmetic, and the figures showed enormous variations. The results, however, were distributed with striking regularity; the differences in the percentages obtained by the different schools of a given community being, for the most part, small.

That the expenditure of time and effort on the part of the pupils should be duly rewarded in some localities and very poorly repaid in others indicates that in some communities a remedy is called for. However, to be effective, the remedy must have an eye to the cause, so that our search for remedial measures must be, in the first instance, directed toward the discovery of the cause of success in some cases and of failure in others. With this in view, it will be necessary to consider the results in the light of each of the elements that enter into the education of the child, as it will not be possible in any other way to find the controlling one.

The number of factors calling for consideration is large. However, the problem may be simplified through classification; and in the preceding chapter

[1] January-March, 1903.

I showed how, in the first instance, it might be divided into two principal parts: (1) The elements relating to the pedagogical side; and (2) those of resistance offered to the influence of the teaching over which the teacher has no direct control. The major portion of that chapter was devoted to a discussion of the second part of the problem, the pupils' side; and I pointed out that the variations in results could not be accounted for by differences in the circumstances under which the teachers labor—differences in the home environment of the pupils, their average age, or the size of the classes; showing that the cause of the variations would have to be sought on the pedagogical side. In the present chapter, I shall direct attention to the latter aspect of the problem, and I believe the discussion will not be fruitless.

The pedagogical side of the problem may also be subdivided into two principal parts: (1) The factors brought into play by the teacher; and (2) the elements relating to those appointed to direct and supervise the work of the teacher. These factors will now be considered in turn.

The elements brought into play by the teacher, though numerous, may be, for practical purposes, resolved into three primary factors:

1. The time devoted to arithmetic;
2. The methods of instruction; and
3. Teaching ability, as represented by a combination of education, training, and the personality of the teacher.

The first of these points received attention in the

preceding chapter; and it was found that the results did not bear a direct relation to the amount of time devoted to arithmetic, so that this element could not be looked upon as the controlling one. I shall here merely recall the fact that the schools whose results were satisfactory proved their ability to do creditable work with a time allotment of forty-five minutes a day, while some of the schools whose results were unsatisfactory failed in spite of a larger appropriation of time.

After my first article on arithmetic appeared in print, the point was raised that the demand in the way of home-work might have been greater in the successful schools than in those that had failed, indicating that, possibly, in some instances, more time had been devoted to arithmetic than showed on the surface. During subsequent visits to the same schools I looked into this matter with considerable care; and I found, much to my surprise, that by far the greatest amount of home-work in arithmetic was required in City VII, whose schools had obtained the poorest results. In this locality, it had constituted an important feature of every grade from the fourth year onward; the requirement in some instances being truly inordinate. On the whole, the average time devoted to it was certainly not less than thirty minutes a day. On the other hand, home-work in arithmetic was looked upon with disfavor by the teachers of all the schools that I have called successful, the first five in the table, and had been practically abandoned in nine cases out of ten.

These facts show conclusively that home-work in

arithmetic is not the controlling factor in the accomplishment of results. Moreover, they ought to carry their lesson to every superintendent in the land. In view of the results and of my interviews with principals and teachers, I feel confident that home-work in arithmetic means a tax upon the time and energy of the pupil for which he receives very meagre, if any, compensation. Consequently, I wish to add to my suggestion, as to the amount of time to be apportioned to arithmetic, that the forty-five minutes daily should stand for the preparation and recitation combined.

Secondly, methods of teaching can certainly not be looked upon as the controlling element. In most schools, the methods nowadays employed are modern, though they may vary in regard to details. In some instances, special methods, based on special psychological theories, had been followed; and while the teachers who used them were, as a rule, enthusiastic in their praise, they did not seem to have proved a panacea. In the schools that passed my test satisfactorily no special methods had been in use.

There is, however, one thing in relation to the teaching of arithmetic that must be regarded as unusually important, and which should receive the attention of every educator. At one point in my investigation I had been led to believe that it was the controlling factor; but further observation compelled me to abandon the notion. The idea is this, that no new step in arithmetic should be taken until all the principles previously acquired are perfectly clear in the minds of the pupils. Where this plan is not observed, the teachers labor upon the theory that the pupils on entering a new grade are perfectly familiar with everything that had been covered in previous grades, and are therefore prepared to enter into the new work without any delay. On the other hand, where the principle is recognized, the teacher of the new grade does not take such knowledge for granted. One seventh-year teacher told me that she does not assume any knowledge on the part of the pupils beyond that of addition, subtraction, multiplication, and division of whole numbers. In such instances, the teacher, on receiving a new class, does not at once begin with the work laid down for her grade, but takes up previous work, chapter by chapter, until she strikes a weak point, where she lingers as long as she thinks necessary. Indeed, I have found a number of schools where the teachers are accustomed to devote several weeks to reviewing the work of previous grades before even touching upon their own grade work. Here progress is apparently slow; but by securing a firm foundation at the outset, the pupils are so much better prepared for the new work that they grasp it much more readily than otherwise, and before the end of the term the grade work is covered without any difficulty. Where the teachers proceed from chapter to chapter without any regard for previous work, the pupils are apt to sail along in a hazy atmosphere; and when taken out of their routine path, they do not know which way to turn.

Thoroughness is, undoubtedly, one of the secrets of success. Indeed, I do not see how success may be expected without it. However, I soon discovered that the review as described does not in itself insure success. Failure in spite of its adoption may be accounted for in two ways. In the first place, the review may be formal, rather than thorough, and therefore lacking in the spirit that makes for success. Secondly, the teacher's work may be thorough without stimulating thought, and the results are not satisfactory unless the pupils are capable of independent thinking. Consequently, something else is required to assure success.

The next point to claim our attention, the qualifications of the teacher, natural and acquired, is popularly regarded as the controlling one; hence the adage, "As the teacher, so is the school." However, that the variations in the results cannot be accounted for by differences in the general qualifications of the teachers is proved by the manner in which the results are distributed. Few will take exception to the statement that marked individual variations will be found among the members of every corps of teachers. Therefore, if general ability were the controlling factor, the extreme variations in results should be found in the different class-rooms of the same locality. But this condition does not appear in the table, where it is shown that in certain localities practically all the results were good, while in certain other cities practically all the results were poor.

It might be argued, in explanation of this circumstance, that, in spite of individual variations, all the teachers of some communities are professionally competent, while in some others they are all incompetent. But this, again, does not accord with the facts; for if a line should be drawn across the table under, say, the seventh school, and the teachers of the communities above it compared with those of the localities below, no marked differences would be noticed. In all the cities represented some teachers may be found who have had both a high-school education and a normal-school training; some who have had a high-school education only; some with much and others with little experience; some with considerable and others with little natural endowment. And as to care in selection, the most favorable conditions will probably be found in Cities IV and VI; and still these localities failed to reach the standard.

We have now exhausted the principal factors brought into play by the teacher, as we have those that belong to the pupil, and as yet the controlling element has not been found. If my investigation is to be rewarded, the object of our search must, therefore, exist among the elements brought into the problem by those employed to supervise and direct the work of the teachers. And the facts have led me to believe that it is here that the controlling factor lies. My conviction is based on the circumstance that, in every instance, a variation in the results appears to accord with a variation in a special phase of the supervision. If my interpretation of the facts is correct, we are forced to conclude that the results secured in the average class-room do not represent the powers of the average teacher, but the response to what is expected of her; so that, ultimately, the problem of results becomes a question of demand and supply. And my deduction is this, that the teachers will supply what their supervisors demand, provided the demand be placed within reasonable bounds. A deduction of this nature is by no means an unnatural one; for it is a matter of common experience that the services rendered by a set of employees are determined by the demands of the management rather than the efficiency of the individuals, assuming, of course, that due care is exercised to see that the demands are enforced. And the facts appear to show that, in this regard, the school does not differ from other institutions.

The leading pedagogical functions of the superintendent, under an ideal system of supervision, may, perhaps, be put down as five in number:

1. The preparation of the course of study;
2. The apportionment of time to the individual subjects;
3. Offering suggestions to teachers, during meetings and visits, as to methods of teaching and the treatment of children;
4. The establishment of demands in regard to results; and
5. The testing for results to see whether the teachers are living up to these demands.

Let us now look into each of these factors and try to find the crucial point.

Owing to differences in educational ideals, the courses laid down for arithmetic vary considerably in different localities. Therefore, it may be argued that, from a comparative standpoint, the results obtained in different communities will depend upon the character of the test; that the pupils of a given locality might do well with one test and poorly with another, and *vice versa*. But, in the preparation of a test to be submitted to different localities, the objection may be allayed by bearing in mind the differences in the course of study, and, in consequence, rejecting all problems of a special character, while selecting from those belonging to general arithmetic, and which, therefore, come within the scope of every school.

The general verdict was that my problems were fair to all. Even in the localities that failed no exception has been taken to my test, which is in itself convincing evidence that the questions did come within the scope of every curriculum. Consequently, the differences in the results cannot be attributed to differences in courses of study. In some instances, it was instinctively felt by superintendents and teachers that the pupils would fail, because the questions were presented in a form differing from that to which the children had been accustomed; and, as a rule, the predictions were verified. In other localities, nothing out of the ordinary was found in the questions; and, as a rule, the schools did well. This did not indicate fundamental differences in ideals, but rather that the work of some schools was more routine in character than that of others; so that the variation in the results showed, primarily, that the pupils of some localities were more ready than those of others in the practical application of principles. In other words, the instruction had done more to stimulate thought in some instances than in others, without regard to fundamental aims.

Another point relating to the course of study also deserves consideration. It is, namely, that in some localities the ground is covered more rapidly than in others, and, therefore, that several of my problems may have come too early for certain schools. This would apply particularly to the seventh-year paper, which contained several rather difficult problems in percentage. To allay all doubts on this score, however, it will be simply necessary to discard the seventh year entirely and take the eighth year as a basis of comparison. But the differences in results in the eighth year were fully as marked as they were in the seventh; and as there was not a problem in the eighth-year paper beyond the scope of any eighth grade, this objection also becomes invalid.

The next point, the amount of time devoted to arithmetic, has been already considered, and requires no further discussion here to prove that this is not the controlling element.

The third point involves that feature of supervision which renders the superintendent an inspirer of teachers, and which, in recent decades, has been receiving an ever increasing amount of attention. In some localities this feature is carried so far as to convert the entire school system into a permanent training school for teachers. Here the superintendent is in constant communication with his teachers, through general and grade meetings and visits to the schools; and when he is imbued with modern pedagogical ideas, his influence on the spirit of the schools is marked, and the atmosphere of the classroom assumes an entirely different character from that which prevails in the old-fashioned, mechanical school. The relation between teacher and pupil is no longer that of master and servant, but resembles rather the relation of parent and child. This spirit is governed by the idea that the pupil is an individual who can think, feel, and act, and not merely a passive recipient of facts. There are many localities in our country where the inspirational system of supervision has been carried to its logical conclusion, and where liberty without license prevails.

But the inspiration of the teachers by the superintendent is not the controlling factor in the accomplishment of results; for superintendents' meetings and visits have been as much in vogue in the localities that did poorly as in those that did well. Consequently, the inspirational element must also be eliminated.

We have now considered all the important factors except the establishment of standards and the testing for results; and these, strictly speaking, merely represent two sides of a single element. As I have already stated, the facts tend to prove that the results are regulated by the demand; and the latter, in my opinion, is represented by the character of the tests to which the pupils are periodically submitted. *This means, in other words, that the controlling factor in the accomplishment of results is to be found in the system of examination employed, some systems leading to better results than others.*

The test, however, has two different meanings, which must not be confounded with each other. In one instance, it is intended to determine the fitness of the pupil for promotion; while in the other its purpose is that of demonstrating the rate and character of the progress made by the class as a whole, *i.e.*, whether the teacher is doing satisfactory work. As the system of testing for promotion has been practically abandoned in every city examined, this factor is common to all, and may, therefore, be here disregarded. As a rule, the pupil's fitness for promotion is now determined by the character of his daily work, supplemented by the teacher's opinion, while the examination as to fitness is reserved for those pupils whose term work has been unsatisfactory or who appeal from the teacher's adverse judgment. *The controlling element lies, therefore, in that form of examination which is intended as a test of the teacher's progress.* The nature of this test varies in different localities; and, as the results appear to vary with its character, a detailed description is called for.

The tests of the teacher's progress may be conveniently summed up in four general classes:

1. Tests made from time to time by the teachers themselves. Each teacher formulates her own questions, marks the papers of her own class, and submits the results to the superintendent; but no tests are made by principal or superintendent.

2. Tests made in the same way by the teachers;

but the teachers' tests are supplemented from time to time by those of the superintendent.

3. Tests made from time to time by the principals, each principal formulating the questions for his own school. The results are reported to the superintendent, but the latter does not make any tests of his own.

4. The same system of testing by the principals; but the principals' tests are supplemented from time to time by those of the superintendent.

The first system means that the demand is fixed by each individual teacher, who is made the judge of her own progress. As the questions prepared by the teacher, when left to her own resources, will naturally accord with the lines upon which she has been teaching, the tendency will be toward routine work. Under these circumstances, the minds of the pupils will be kept running in a groove, in which they may work with remarkable facility, but outside of which they are all at sea. In other words, the pupils will be able to solve certain problems without any difficulty when they are presented in the customary way, but entirely incapable of solving them when they are stated in a different manner. I was once present in a class-room when a pupil was called upon to analyze a problem in mental arithmetic. He rose to his feet, but was silent. After the teacher had waited a little while, she said to the child: "Don't you know? That's the kind that begins with 'since.'" This suggestion was sufficient to enable the pupil to go through the analysis according to rule. Such methods as this will account for the fact that a class which will regularly obtain an average of 80 to 90 per cent on the teacher's test may obtain less than 20 per cent on a test such as my own.

The plan of limiting the tests to those of the teacher has been in vogue in City VI, and the results may be judged by a glance at the table. I could find no other element in this locality to account for the failure. In fact, in every way the conditions are here above the average. The home surroundings of the pupils are, for the most part, favorable; the classes are small; the teachers are selected with more than ordinary care; and the superintendent does his share from the inspirational standpoint. The only thing that seems to be lacking is the test from a broader point of view than that of the teacher. If the superintendent would inaugurate a system of examinations of a different order, there is little doubt in my mind that in the course of a year or two the results in arithmetic would be improved by at least 50 per cent. In City IV also the conditions are favorable, but the testing is not very systematic.

Under the second system, the degree of success seems to depend upon the nature of the tests prepared by the superintendent. If he should not demand anything beyond a fair knowledge of the term's work at the end of the term, and if he should have an eye to principles rather than ingenuity in their application, his tests may be as routine as those of the teacher, and fail to exert a stimulating influence. This criticism applies to City VII, where the second plan of examinations has been in vogue; and when my own test was here placed before the pupils, the result was chaos. The superintendent and teachers seemed at once to appreciate the nature of the difficulty; and they feel confident that if I should try their schools again, after giving them a little chance to wake up, they would be able to show much better results. In another locality, the principal of a school that failed attributed the failure to the routine character of the tests to which his pupils had been accustomed.

Under the third system, the tests are made by the principal, instead of the teacher, thus bringing into play a broader point of view than the first plan. It has the advantage that, in the first instance, it is not the teacher herself, but the principal, who is made the judge of the teacher's progress; but, lacking the superintendent's test, the system has the weakness of making the principal the judge of the progress of his own school. This indicates simply that the tests will represent the demands of the individual principals. The principal of a given school may be petty, and guided by the desire to make a good showing, or he may lack the proper perspective. In either case, the tests may run along routine lines, with an eye to grade work, and bring forth marvellous percentages from pupils who would fail completely on tests requiring independent thought. On the other hand, the principal may be a man of broad calibre, or an original genius, whose primary aim does not exist in the endeavor to show high percentages, but in stimulating pupils to use their minds. His tests will call for independent thought, and they cannot be passed unless the teachers have taught the pupils to think for themselves. The percentages brought out by his tests may not be nearly so high as those obtained in the school just described; so that, in the superintendent's records, his school may stand much lower than the other. However, when a test is applied which calls for thought, rather than form, his pupils will not be mentally paralyzed, and their previous training will tell. The eighth-grade teacher of the school at the head of the table—a school where the tests are made by the principal—told me that she did not think my problems fair, because they did not test the power of her pupils. She was not at all proud of them because her class averaged 91 per cent. She thought they should have done much better than that. And she was not inclined to change her mind when she learned that the eighth grade in many of the schools did not average 30 per cent. The principal of this school is constantly after the pupils, who are, therefore, at all times, ready for the unusual.

In localities where the principal is made the judge of his own progress, he becomes a very important factor in the school system. Indeed, in one sense, he assumes the functions of a superintendent. To this there can be no valid objection; for the superintendent, especially in the larger cities, cannot come into close touch with every class-room. However, under this plan the tendency will be toward the development of great inequalities in the different schools of the same community; each school representing the proclivities of its principal, rather than those of the city superintendent.

The fourth system differs from the third in this only, that the independent tests of the principal are supplemented once or twice a year by uniform tests prepared by the superintendent. Here the principal is not left entirely to his own resources, but, from time to time, is himself subjected to a test. The advantage of this plan lies in the fact that it is capable of bringing to light the comparative progress of the different schools, which is not the case when the results reported to the superintendent from the various schools are based on tests of varying degrees of difficulty. The knowledge on the part of the principal that his school is to be judged by tests other than his own cannot fail to exert an influence on the nature of the tests prepared by himself, which will be guided by the character of those submitted by the superintendent. If the latter call for independent thought, the principals must see that the teachers will train their pupils to think; otherwise their schools will not be likely to make a good showing. Even under these conditions some of the schools will fail, because the principals themselves are not equally competent or equally ambitious; but the tendency will be to stimulate those who are ambitious, and who wish to stand well among their colleagues. Therefore, the best principals of the town will be likely to do better work, and among the less competent the number of failures will be smaller. This system of examination describes, in a general way, the plan in vogue in City I.

In the foregoing I have attempted to point out, first, why some schools succeeded in passing my test and others failed; and, secondly, what mode of procedure, according to the facts, is destined to lead to the most favorable results. However, I do not wish to convey the impression that I claim to have solved the educational problem. I fully believe that my data, though comparatively meagre, justify the deduction that, other things being equal, the results obtained by the teacher will vary with the demand, which simply shows a further application of a very well-recognized fundamental law. Further investigations may prove that I am wrong, and that the controlling factor is an altogether different one.

But taking it for granted, for the sake of argument, that my deduction is correct, this does not indicate that I have really solved the problem. If we are willing to accept the statement that the results are controlled by the demand, we are simply carried to the threshold of another, and much larger, problem. Assuming the organization of a school system to be ideal, that is, that the principal is broader than his teachers, and that the superintendent is broader than his principals, then the deduction is logical that it is fitting for the demand to be fixed by the superintendent. This, however, merely leads us to the question: What principles shall guide the superintendent in formulating his demands? He must ask neither too much nor too little of his teachers. If he asks too much, the consequence will be a waste of effort in the attempt to do the impossible. On the other hand, if he asks too little, the pupils will not be sufficiently taxed to develop the best that is in them.

But how is the superintendent to determine the mean? Thus far no higher law has been recognized than that of personal opinion; so that all standards now in existence are purely arbitrary in their nature. Nevertheless, there is a higher law, and one which will have to be brought to bear on the educational problem, if permanent progress is looked for. The law is this, that the demand must be based on the normal mental capacity of the child, that is, on a knowledge of what the average child [1] who has been well taught is capable of doing in an individual branch, at a given period of school-life, when a given amount of time has been devoted to that branch. This is not a question of opinion, but a question of fact, a problem whose solution depends upon extended investigations.

If we look over the pedagogical field to get our bearings from the standpoint of the mental capacity of the child, we can find as yet no definite landmarks to serve as guides in the establishment of standards. Under these circumstances, the superintendent's demands cannot be representative of anything more definite than his personal opinion—a condition that must necessarily prevail until a more or less substantial literature on the child's capacity has been developed. In the meantime our educators must resort to expedients; and, for the present, the wisest course, it seems to me, lies in the adoption of a system of examinations as outlined in plan number four.

[1] Recognizing that no two individuals are alike, some educators take exception to the term "average child." However, there can be no objection if we accept it in a figurative sense, taking the class as a unit.

However, the mere inauguration of a fruitful system of examinations does not itself insure success. As I have already stated, the nature of the results will be determined, for the most part, by the character of the tests prepared by the superintendent. If the problems do not call for independent thought, and if they can be solved without any difficulty should the teacher have devoted her entire attention to drilling the pupils in the work of her own grade, then the tests of the principal will follow this lead, and the examinations will be as routine in character as those which are made by the teachers themselves, in accordance with plan number one. To be of the highest value, the superintendent's questions must be suggestive and stimulating, both to the principals and the teachers. They must aim to take the latter out of the groove, and be so formulated that they will call for a thorough grasp of the entire subject as far as the pupils have advanced, as well as a readiness on the part of the latter to comprehend a problem that comes within their scope, regardless of how it is stated. When I say that the standard implied by a test of this nature is not an impossible one, and that its attainment is purely a matter of training, I am not merely expressing a personal opinion, but I am speaking from actual facts—as witness, in the table, 81 per cent against 8 in the seventh year, and 91 per cent against 11 in the eighth.

A further illustration of the same fact was given a few weeks ago when I submitted an apparently simple, but rather puzzling, little problem to the pupils of the eighth year of a number of schools. In one instance, where the pupils had failed on my general test, the class average on this little problem was 10 per cent only. I asked the teacher how she accounted for the failure, and her reply was: "Children don't think." If she had spoken more truly, she would have said: "These children don't think," or "My pupils have not been trained to think"; for in another instance, in the school that stood first on my general test, the class average on the same problem was as high as 60 per cent. It might be argued that, perhaps, in the one school the pupils had previously had problems similar to the one I gave, while in the other they had not. This is just the point. If not, why not? In some schools it is difficult to find practical problems that are not in line with previous work; and, therefore, almost any practical question seems quite familiar to the pupils. But in other schools the pupils seem to be able to look in one direction only, so that questions from other points of view represent to them merely so many Chinese puzzles.

The conclusion that the controlling factor in the accomplishment of results is to be found among the duties of the superintendent may be open to the criticism that I started out with a theory, and that, in interpreting my data, I was influenced by the desire to prove my theory—a form of criticism to which investigators are not infrequently subjected. However, to this charge I must enter the plea, "Not guilty." That I have had, for some time, a rather strong leaning in a certain direction, I shall not deny.

But my belief was that the variations in the results were due, primarily, to differences in the personality and qualifications of teachers—a theory which the facts compelled me to abandon. And I did not see what I now believe to be the controlling factor until every element I had mentioned had been critically examined and found wanting.

It is gratifying to me to be able to say that the facts were not interpreted in the light of the conclusion, but that the conclusion was formed in the light of the facts. Nevertheless, when I recall my educational experiences of a decade ago, I am somewhat surprised that my impressions did not favor, from the outset, the theory to which the facts have led me. In January, 1892, after spending considerable time in studying the school systems abroad, I entered into an agreement with *The Forum* to visit the schools of our own country, and to prepare a series of articles embodying my observations. I started out early in January of that year, and traveled continuously for over five months, during which time I had an opportunity to visit schools in session in thirty-six cities, and to consult a large number of superintendents, teachers, and others more or less directly interested in education. At the end of that period I felt that I was ready to express some opinions, and the publication of my series began in October, 1892, and did not close until June, 1893.

It was not my purpose at the time to study the results of instruction, but rather the spirit of the schools. I had long believed that elementary education should take into account the normal activities and interests of the child; that the latter should be introduced to the beauties of nature and art; and that he should be as free in his schoolroom as orderly development would permit. From the standpoint of spirit and breadth of curriculum, I found all sorts and conditions of schools. In many localities, the sitting-still school, with all its mechanical appurtenances, still flourished; in some, the endeavor to break away from the old-fashioned, mechanical grind was in evidence; and in not a few instances I found localities where my idle fancies had been more than realized.

The most striking feature of my observations was the fact that, from the standpoint of spirit, any one school of a given locality was, broadly speaking, representative of the schools of its locality as a whole. When the repression of the child was found in the first school that I visited, it was found in the other schools as well; and, in the same way, when in the first school I found spontaneity, it was an indication that I should find freedom in the other schools also. This was strong evidence to the effect that the spirit of the schools of every locality must be controlled by a central authority; and the accumulated data led me to the conclusion that the tone of the class-room was representative of the personality of the superintendent, provided he had had charge of the schools long enough to make his personality felt. And this conclusion, I believe, has stood the test of time. The term superintendent is here used in the larger sense, which includes the members of his staff.

From the deduction stated the inference is natural: "If the superintendent is responsible for the spirit of the schools, why is he not also responsible for the results?" If the superintendent wishes to develop a good school spirit, it is necessary for him to work for spirit. If he is desirous of accomplishing results of a high order, it is necessary for him to work for results.

In view of what I have said, the aim of supervision is clearly a double one. In the first place, the superintendent must see that a wholesome spirit is developed in the schools; and, secondly, it is also his duty to see that due attention is paid to results. This again gives rise to an important question: Is it possible to keep the results in view without at the same time crushing the spirit? Or, conversely, Is it possible to develop a delightful class-room atmosphere without at the same time destroying the results?

Judging by my own impressions, acquired by a twofold study of the question, spirit and results are in no way incompatible. The criticism aimed at the modern school spirit, that it means a milk-and-water system, a weak sentimentality rather than mental discipline of a wholesome kind, does, perhaps, apply to the schools of those localities where the mere utterance of the word "results" is looked upon as sacrilegious—schools that are in a transitional stage, just emerging from an antiquated system, and not yet accustomed to their new surroundings. But the criticism does not apply to localities where a good spirit has already become an established fact, and additional aims can be held in view without losing sight of the fundamental proposition. In itself, a good school spirit does not indicate weakness any more than a poor spirit is an indication of strength. In some of the delightful schools, it is true, the results are by no means praiseworthy; but, on the other hand, the results are frequently of a very inferior order in typical schools of the antiquated kind.

There is, indeed, no logical reason why results may not be kept in view without in any way neglecting the spirit; for "subjects" are taught in the modern as well as in the antiquated schools, and the time devoted to the formal studies is, in most instances, ample to lead to satisfactory results. If the modern idea should stand for the abandonment of the three R's, it might be deemed unworthy; but it does nothing of the kind. The matter simply resolves itself into a question like this: "All other things being equal, will forty-five minutes a day devoted to arithmetic in the schools in which the pupils are active and responsive accomplish as much as forty-five minutes devoted to arithmetic in the schools where the pupils are repressed and passive?" The facts compel us to answer this question in the affirmative. Therefore, there is no reason to doubt that a good school spirit and satisfactory results may without difficulty go hand in hand.

IX

TALENT VS. TRAINING IN TEACHING.[1] ARITHMETIC CONCLUDED

In Chapter VII, I presented the results of a test in arithmetic. The test had been submitted to the pupils of the fourth, fifth, sixth, seventh, and eighth year classes in eighteen school buildings, representing seven cities, and the total number of children examined was not far from six thousand. While the figures obtained were surprising in many ways, they were particularly so in these two points: (1) That the results obtained in the different schools varied to a remarkable extent, the averages per school ranging from 25 to 80 per cent; and (2) that when the schools were listed in the order of merit, those of an individual locality were, with a single exception, so close together that the results obtained in a given school were, to a large extent, representative of all the schools examined in that locality. In other words, when the results were good in one building they were good in other buildings examined in the same locality; and the same was true where they were fair or poor.

In addition to the study of results, I entered into a detailed inquiry concerning the conditions under

[1] April-June, 1903.

which the results had been obtained, in the hope of finding the cause or causes of success or of failure. Among the points considered were the age and home environment of the pupils, the size of each class, the methods of instruction, the qualifications of the teachers, natural and acquired, the time devoted to arithmetic, and the character of the supervision. A study of the results from these various points of view led me to the conclusion stated in Chapter VIII, namely, that the controlling element in the achievement of success lay in a single phase of supervision, that is, in the training afforded to the teacher through systematically testing the progress of her pupils by means of examinations consisting of problems that cannot be solved unless the children thoroughly understand the principles of arithmetic—from the beginning of the subject up to the time the examination is given—and are possessed of the power of applying them.

After the appearance of my second article on arithmetic (Chapter VIII), two important points were raised in criticism of my deductions; and, for the sake of throwing light on the subject from additional points of view, I shall devote the present chapter to answering them. They are:

1. That in placing the responsibility for the results primarily upon the supervision, I had underestimated the value of the personality of the teacher; and

2. That a single test will not suffice to bring out the comparative strength of the pupils; that the ideals in arithmetic differ in different communities;

and that if the test had been of a different character, the order of merit might have been reversed.

In regard to the first point, I desire to impress not only the fact that my conclusion was based upon the results, but also that it does not in any way conflict with generally accepted pedagogical views. Indeed, all advanced educational legislation is based upon the belief that pedagogical talent, like any other talent, is subject to development through training. In evidence of this we find not only that institutions for the training of teachers are growing more and more in favor, but that our elementary school systems are planned upon the idea of the need of continuous training. Hence, our supervising principals, special supervisors, and superintendents of schools. At the same time, it cannot be doubted that natural endowment is of inestimable value in teaching, as in every other field; so that the question at issue really resolves itself into that of the relative value of talent and training. That this question may be studied from the standpoint of statistics, I have, in Table I (p. 156), arranged the figures in a way that will show the influence of the personality of the teacher as compared with that of training; but before entering into the discussion of that table, I shall cite a few instances to illustrate that even from a theoretical standpoint a deficiency in talent can be overcome by training.

Let us first imagine two individuals, one of whom is a pedagogical genius, while the other is absolutely devoid of the pedagogical instinct. In this case, there is little doubt that the former would always be the better teacher, even if she should have no training whatever, and the latter should have the benefit of the most thorough training that the world can afford.

Next, let us imagine two individuals one of whom is not really a genius, but whose pedagogical talent is considerable, represented, say, by 75 per cent, while the other is not altogether pedagogically weak, but possesses native ability to the extent of 25 per cent. Under these circumstances, it is not at all impossible to conceive of conditions under which the efficiency of the latter could rise to the level of that of the former. If both these individuals should pass through the same course of training before receiving their licenses to teach, and then should secure positions in the same school building, *i.e.*, under the same principal and superintendent, it is quite rational to assume that their relative native efficiency would tell, and that the work of the one would always be far superior to that of the other. But if, after receiving their licenses, the young lady with considerable talent should obtain a position in a school where the principal and the superintendent permitted her to drift, while the other should enter a system where the superintendent was vigilant, and a building whose principal was not only a thoughtful and tireless worker, but in addition had a genius for developing the best that was in his teachers, is it not conceivable that, in time, the teacher who had been permitted to drift would accomplish less than her native talent would warrant, showing an efficiency of not more than 50 per cent, while the teacher who had been put on her mettle would so have developed her native ability that her efficiency would have risen to 50 per cent?

And, thirdly, let us imagine two teachers whose native efficiencies were 60 and 40—and these are really representative of the average persons who enter the profession—is it not conceivable that, under the conditions just outlined, the efficiency of the former, who had no specially marked bent for teaching, would fall to 30, while that of the other, who was not particularly weak at the outset, would rise to 70, so that at the end of a given period the odds would be strongly in favor of the teacher who had started out in life with less in her favor?

That, in this instance, theory is duly borne out by the facts is very strikingly indicated in Table I, which shows, side by side, the influence of the teacher's personality as compared with that of the system of schools in which she is employed. The figures represent, first, the results obtained in every class-room of the four schools examined in City I, where the test of the character described is used by both the superintendent and the principal; secondly, those obtained in the three schools of City VI, where no tests are made by superintendent or principal; and, thirdly, those secured in the three schools of City VII, where tests are made by the superintendent, but the problems are limited to the grade work of the class.

That the personality of the teacher is not the controlling element in the achievement of success is, in my opinion, amply proved by the fact that in

Cities VI and VII the results, with few exceptions, fell below a reasonable standard in every class-

TABLE I

4			5			6			7			8		
City I.	City VI.	City VII.	City I.	City VI.	City VII.	City I.	City VI.	City VII.	City I.	City VI.	City VII.	City I.	City VI.	City VII.
....	....	....	85.6	....	....	88.8	....	....	....	....	....	86.6	....	....
....	....	....	85.3	....	....	....	....	....	....	....	....	....	....	....
83.0	....	....	84.9	....	....	81.5	....	....	....	....	....	80.9	....	....
....	....	....	83.5	....	....	....	....	....	....	....	....	....	....	....
....	....	....	....	....	81.2	....	....	....	....	....	....	....	....	....
....	....	....	79.0	....	....	79.4	....	....	....	....	....	....	....	....
....	....	....	77.8	....	....	....	....	....	....	....	....	....	....	....
72.4	....	....	75.0	....	....	72.4	....	....	....	....	....	72.7	....	....
....	....	....	74.6	....	....	72.2	....	....	....	....	....	....	....	....
....	....	....	71.1	....	....	71.1	....	....	71.7	....	....	....	....	....
63.3	....	....	66.8	....	....	....	68.3	....	65.1	....	....	66.5	....	....
62.7	....	....	....	....	....	67.1	....	....	62.0	....	....	61.0	....	....
....	....	59.3	....	....	....	....	....	....	....	....	....	....	....	....
56.8	....	....	....	55.0	55.1	....	....	....	58.3	....	....	....	....	....
56.4	....	....	....	....	....	....	....	....	....	....	....	....	....	....
51.8	....	....	....	....	52.4	....	....	....	54.6	....	....	....	....	....
....	....	....	....	....	....	....	46.1	....	....	....	....	....	....	....
....	....	47.4	....	....	49.6	....	46.0	....	48.8	....	....	....	....	....
....	41.6	41.1	....	45.3	....	....	....	40.2	41.7	....	....	....	....	....
....	36.8	....	....	38.1	....	....	34.5	34.0	....	33.5	....	....	35.2	....
....	....	....	....	....	37.5	....	....	....	....	30.5	....	....	....	30.0
....	....	....	....	....	....	....	....	....	....	....	....	....	26.9	....
....	28.1	....	....	....	....	....	....	27.6	....	....	29.7	....	23.3	....
....	....	....	....	...	....	....	....	27.3	....	....	....	....	....	21.6
....	....	....	....	....	....	....	....	26.5	....	....	....	....	....	20.4
....	....	....	....	....	....	....	....	....	....	19.5	19.6	....	....	....
....	....	....	....	....	....	....	....	....	....	....	17.3	....	....	....
....	....	....	....	....	....	....	....	....	....	....	10.0	....	....	18.9
....	....	....	....	....	....	....	....	....	....	....	8.9	....	....	11.3

room examined, while in City I, with few exceptions, they rose above that standard. However, the figures do not show that nothing is to be credited to the personality of the teacher; for while in Cities VI and VII the results, on the whole, were low, they were not equally low; and, on the other hand, although, in general, the results in City I were high, they were not equally high. That is to say, differences in percentages allowing for differences in the personality of the teachers were well marked in all these cities, but the results were on a different plane. The scope representing the teacher's personality is represented by the differences in the individual columns, *i.e.*, by the percentages obtained in the different class-rooms of the same grade in any one locality, while the influence of the school-system as a whole is seen when the figures of one column are compared with those of another.

Taking the individual columns of grade 4, we find that in City I the class averages run from 51.8 to 83, showing an extreme variation of 31.2; in City VI, they vary from 28.1 to 41.6; and in City VII, from 41.1 to 59.3. If we now compare the figures of one column with those of another, we can see the influence of the system; and by drawing a line across the three columns of grade 4 at 50, we find that all the classes examined in City I are above it, while, with a single exception, all those of Cities VI and VII are below.

In the 5th grade, barring a single instance, the poorest grade average of City I is 11.8 per cent higher than the best of Cities VI and VII, and 29.3 higher than the poorest. In the 6th grade, again leaving out an exceptional instance, the poorest average in City I is 21 per cent higher than the best of Cities VI and VII, and 40.6 per cent higher than the poorest. In the 7th grade there is no exception, the lowest average in City I being 8.2 per cent better than the highest in the other cities, and 32.8 per cent better than the lowest. And in the 8th grade of City I, the lowest average is 25.8 per cent better than the highest in the other cities, and 49.7 per cent better than the lowest.

Looking at the matter from another point of view, we find that in 30 class-rooms out of the 33 examined in Cities VI and VII, the highest marks were below the poorest obtained in the 38 class-rooms examined in City I.[1] But the influence of the system is brought out most strikingly when the lowest averages of Cities VI and VII are compared with the lowest of City I, as this shows most directly the general uplift given by something in the latter's system, which I believe to be the stimulating test.

It may be believed that some of the questions were too difficult for grades 4, 6, and 7. If so, we may leave these grades out of consideration, and confine our attention to the 5th and the 8th, where the problems should not have been beyond the pupils. But this does not change in any way the comparative standing of the schools represented.

In spite of the figures, it is difficult to say just how many counts out of 100 should be attributed to the personality of the teacher and how many counts to the system. The differences are, perhaps, as marked in the columns which allow for the one as they are in the comparisons representing the other. But the variations in the individual columns

[1] To avoid needless overcrowding of the column, two class-rooms, averaging 77.1 and 71 respectively, were omitted from City I, grade 5.

do not represent the influence of the teacher's personality alone. Here allowance must be made for another important factor, namely, the differences in the ability of the classes, which are sometimes very marked.

But the potency of the system is clearly indicated by the fact that under its influence the poorest teachers will be able to make some kind of a showing with the poorest of classes. Taking City I, we find that while in the 4th grade three of the classes fell below 60, not one of them fell below 50; and that while two classes in the 7th grade fell below 50, not one of them fell below 40, although the 7th year test proved to have been exceptionally severe. In the 5th and the 8th grades, where the suitability of the questions can scarcely be doubted, the lowest averages in City I were 66.8 and 61, respectively, against 37.5 and 11.3. Taken all in all, I do not think I exaggerate when I say that the system is the equivalent of 25 counts. That is to say, speaking from my own deductions, I am inclined to believe that if Cities VI and VII should introduce a system of testing similar to that employed in City I, and its introduction should be accompanied by a specific demand upon the principals and teachers, it would not be very long before a test equally difficult as my own would result in school averages of 60 to 65 per cent, in place of 35 to 40 per cent, as was the case when these schools were examined a year ago.

From the foregoing analysis, I believe we are justified in concluding that the question of the relative value of talent and training has a theoretical and a practical side. From a theoretical point of view, I am willing to concede in favor of personality even more than the figures show, and to go so far as to say that one who is exceptionally endowed by nature is able to rise above her surroundings, and can do as well if left to her own resources as under the closest of supervision. The figures do not do justice to this teacher, because she is simply a link in a chain, and the pupils may enter her classroom so poorly prepared that it will require a herculean effort even on her part to raise them merely to a moderate degree of proficiency.

From a practical point of view, however, the situation seems to be controlled by the training afforded by that form of supervision which tends to stimulate the teacher to do her best, because the vast majority of the teachers are persons of moderate ability, who are in need of a stimulus from an outside source if they are to do the best work of which they are capable. And, taking a community as a whole, the support afforded by such a stimulus as an ideal system of testing—in which the superintendent and the principal are factors of equal importance—seems to be sufficient to raise considerably the efficiency of the entire corps. The teachers' meeting is valuable, because it gives the teacher ideas; but the meeting must be supplemented by the test, in order that the superintendent may be assured that the ideas acquired at the meetings are afterward applied in practice.

I desire to add here that in the present stage of

our pedagogical knowledge, when we are guided altogether by theory, poor results in a given locality do not in any way speak against the efficiency of the superintendent. Wide-awake superintendents are in the habit of following the trend of advancing pedagogical thought; and if that trend is in the wrong direction, the superintendent is not responsible. The tendency for some years past has been for example, to oppose examinations of every form; and, in view of this circumstance, the superintendent has been fully justified in abandoning them. If, however, further investigations should substantiate my contention, and facts should prove the examination to be a *sine qua non*, then the tests will probably be the most speedily reintroduced by the very men who were most ready to set them aside. It is in questions of this kind, where strong forces are arrayed on both sides, that the value of educational research is most clearly apparent; for some of the most practical points of school administration upon which agreement cannot be reached through opinions may be decided without difficulty by statistics.

Let us now direct our attention to the second point, and endeavor to learn whether the results obtained by my test are representative of the comparative strength of the schools examined, or whether a test of a different nature, based upon different ideals, might have shown strength where weakness was manifested, and *vice versa*.

In formulating my problems, I did not lose sight of the fact that the courses in arithmetic vary in different communities; and I therefore endeavored to secure questions that would call for a knowledge of arithmetic such as would naturally come within the scope of all schools, regardless of what their ideals might be. In spite of my precautions, it is possible that some of the problems were beyond the scope of certain schools. If so, the matter can be easily remedied by eliminating them and drawing our conclusions from the others. But just as the exclusion of certain grades in their entirety would fail to alter the relative positions of the schools, so the exclusion of certain selected problems would not alter their relative positions.

In order that the comparisons may be made by the reader from a very broad point of view, I shall place before him, first, the results that were obtained on each example in the five schools that passed the test satisfactorily and those obtained in the lowest six. And, secondly, I shall enter into the analysis of a sufficient number of the problems to show wherein the examination was characteristic and in what manner the pupils went astray in their work. The classification of the errors will show that, at least in the majority of instances, the mistakes in the lower grades were due to lack of judgment in the application of elementary principles, while in the upper grades they were due, for the most part, to a lack of knowledge of the principles involved. The errors made by the pupils in the stronger schools were exactly the same in character as those made in the weaker ones, the difference being simply in the number of pupils who failed.

The results obtained on the individual problems

TABLE 2

Fourth Grade.	Class Average.		1. Children in New York Schools.		2. Profit on House and Lot.		3. Balance for Farm.		4. Number Acres in Farm.		5. Change from $10.		6. Cream.		7. Papers.		8. Pencils.	
	Result.	Princi-ple.	Result.	Princi-ple.	Result.	Princi-ple.	Result.	Princi-ple.	Result.	Princi-ple.	Result.	Princi-ple.	Result.	Princi-ple.	Result.	Princi-ple.	Result.	Princi-ple.
City VI	35.7	46.6	51.9	82.3	59.8	67.6	38.2	49.0	34.2	50.0	30.3	44.1	30.3	33.3	33.3	36.2	10.7	15.6
City VII	50.6	60.8	49.4	69.4	76.8	83.1	64.2	76.8	73.6	85.2	53.6	81.0	28.4	30.5	45.2	46.3	13.6	14.7
City I	64.7	75.0	69.5	85.5	82.2	91.2	74.6	86.1	76.8	84.0	56.0	88.8	71.6	72.8	56.6	60.2	30.7	34.0
City III, School 1	68.4	76.7	68.9	91.1	83.9	90.6	80.8	92.2	74.6	75.1	66.3	84.4	81.8	81.8	60.1	62.7	31.6	35.2
General average — all schools examined	59.5	69.9	66.6	87.1	79.5	86.9	70.1	82.8	69.4	80.0	52.8	76.5	60.3	61.9	51.6	55.3	27.5	31.8

TABLE 3

Fifth Grade.	Class Average.		Profit on House and Lot.		Length of Tel. Wire.		Number of Dress Patterns.		Cream.		Papers.		Pencils.		Profit on Flour.		Cost of Book.	
	Result.	Princi-ple.	Result.	Princi-ple.	Result.	Princi-ple.	Result.	Princi-ple.	Result.	Princi-ple.	Result.	Princi-ple.	Result.	Princi-ple.	Result.	Princi-ple.	Result.	Princi-ple.
City VI	45.6	52.5	75.8	87.0	62.9	75.9	56.8	62.0	46.3	48.2	47.4	49.1	31.8	33.6	22.4	32.7	22.4	31.8
City VII	56.2	63.7	81.0	93.1	79.0	90.5	64.1	67.5	64.1	64.8	64.1	68.2	32.4	37.8	34.4	45.2	30.6	41.8
City III, No. 1	79.5	82.5	95.6	97.8	80.1	88.7	83.2	83.8	87.6	88.7	80.1	80.1	77.9	81.1	67.7	70.9	63.4	69.3
City I	78.0	83.8	94.3	97.2	86.3	91.8	90.0	94.9	88.9	90.6	81.7	83.8	70.0	76.0	61.6	74.7	53.5	61.4
General average — all schools examined	69.4	75.5	89.5	95.6	80.3	90.1	77.1	83.1	80.4	81.4	73.6	76.3	58.7	63.2	49.8	59.0	47.5	56.0

in the schools mentioned will be found in Tables 2 to 5. Two percentages are given upon each example. The first represents the number of correct answers, while the second represents the problems correctly performed in principle, but wherein mechanical errors led to wrong results. For the sake of clearness, the problems have been arranged in the order of difficulty as manifested by the test, not that in which they were presented to the pupils. For facility of reference, each problem is indicated in the tables by a suggestive word or two. The questions were printed in their original order at the close of Chapter VII.

Now, if the question of ideals should play a part in the comparative standing of the schools, the comparative degree of difficulty of the various problems should be found to vary in different localities according to the special lines along which they had been working. It ought to be found that while, on the whole, some of the schools fell far behind the others, they nevertheless manifested superiority in certain directions, and would have outranked the others on a test based more generally upon those lines. On looking over the tables, however, such a condition is in no wise manifested. On the contrary, the tables speak forcibly against such an assumption, and in two ways: First, they show that the schools that passed the test satisfactorily outranked the others on every problem, and in many instances to a very large degree. And, secondly, the figures are still more striking in that they show that, broadly speaking, the comparative degree of

TABLE 4

Sixth Grade.	Class Average.		Cream.		Papers.		Pencils.		Profit on Flour.		Buffalo to Omaha.		Salt Water.		Map.		Number of Books in Library.	
	Result.	Principle.	Result.	Principle.	Result.	Principle.	Result.	Principle.	Result.	Principle.	Result.	Principle.	Result.	Principle.	Result.	Principle.	Result.	Principle.
City VII..................	32.1	37.1	67.0	68.2	54.2	57.3	52.4	60.3	38.4	62.8	29.8	33.5	11.5	11.5	3.6	3.6	0	0
City VI..................	46.0	49.3	67.5	67.5	59.7	64.9	51.9	53.2	51.9	59.7	64.9	68.8	25.8	28.5	25.8	25.8	19.4	9.4
City I..................	76.2	78.5	96.8	97.2	94.8	94.8	89.6	91.3	86.5	92.7	88.9	89.9	50.8	56.4	33.2	34.6	49.1	49.1
City III, No. 1.........	79.3	80.3	99.2	99.2	100	100	96.2	97.3	93.2	94.7	93.9	93.9	45.1	49.6	63.9	64.6	43.6	43.6
General average — all schools examined.....	60.7	63.2	89.8	90.2	85.2	86.4	77.9	80.7	69.9	79.4	72.0	74.3	32.7	36.8	29.5	29.6	22.7	22.7

TABLE 5

Seventh Grade.	Class Average.		Butter.		Salt Water.		Map.		Coffee.		Number of Books in Library.		Steel.		Fruit.		Weaving.	
	Result.	Principle.	Result.	Principle.	Result.	Principle.	Result.	Principle.	Result.	Principle.	Result.	Principle.	Result.	Principle.	Result.	Principle.	Result.	Principle.
City VII..................	18.0	20.0	58.7	64.3	47.7	49.2	15.1	15.1	12.1	12.1	9.8	9.8	5.3	7.5	0	0	0.7	1.5
City VI..................	26.4	30.8	59.4	79.7	35.1	43.2	33.7	37.8	36.4	36.4	24.3	24.3	14.8	21.6	5.4	5.4	5.4	6.7
City I..................	56.7	60.3	75.2	88.0	61.0	71.1	42.2	43.1	72.9	72.9	74.7	75.2	50.9	53.2	52.7	54.1	22.4	24.7
City III, No. 1	81.1	82.3	88.1	96.6	91.5	91.5	98.8	98.3	94.9	96.6	83.0	83.0	74.5	74.5	69.4	69.4	49.1	49.1
General average — all schools examined.....	39.4	42.5	67.4	80.5	52.3	56.5	41.9	42.6	41.5	42.0	38.8	39.1	25.2	26.7	24.0	25.4	16.5	17.5

TABLE 5

Eighth Grade.	Class Average.		1. Salt Water.		2. Map.		3. Number of Books in Library.		4. Gunpowder.		5. Insurance.		6. Steel.		7. Horses.		8. Fruit.	
	Result.	Princi-ple.	Result.	Princi-ple.	Result.	Princi-ple.	Result.	Princi-ple.	Result.	Princi-ple.	Result.	Princi-ple.	Result.	Princi-ple.	Result.	Princi-ple.	Result.	Princi-ple.
City VII	20.1	21.5	60.5	60.5	32.1	32.1	18.9	18.9	25.5	30.6	5.8	6.5	5.1	5.1	4.3	5.1	4.3	8.7
City VI	28.6	30.7	58.8	58.3	31.2	33.3	25.0	25.0	16.6	16.6	22.9	27.1	16.6	20.8	25.0	27.0	33.3	33.3
City I	73.9	77.2	75.1	84.0	93.7	94.2	88.0	88.0	84.5	88.0	65.7	75.4	68.0	68.0	66.8	68.0	50.5	52.5
City III, No. 1	91.7	93.9	85.7	85.7	100	100	97.1	97.1	97.1	100	94.2	94.2	88.5	88.5	91.1	91.1	80.0	94.2
General average — all schools examined	49.4	51.9	70.1	72.5	67.1	67.4	57.2	57.2	51.7	54.6	39.1	43.8	38.2	38.8	36.7	38.0	29.5	33.1

difficulty of the various examples was found to be the same in every locality; indicating that work along special lines, if such there was, did not tell in a test of judgment. The decline in the percentages from the first problem to the eighth is especially marked in the upper two lines; the occasional elevations or depressions following no general rule. It is most clearly marked in the first line of Table 5, where the descent resembles a veritable avalanche.

The tables are instructive from another standpoint, namely, as indicating the child's capacity for arithmetic at different periods of school life, thus aiding in the development of standards. In regard to the mental powers of children, teachers are altogether too apt to generalize upon the basis of what their own pupils are able to do; and when a teacher is not successful, she is apt to think but little of children's minds. Lines 3 and 4 of the tables indicated show that children can reason, and that their reasoning powers, as regards arithmetic, are capable of development to a remarkable degree through training.

As to the variety of errors, these may be most conveniently studied under certain general classifications. Although the number of groups into which they could be divided is almost without limit, nevertheless, if we disregard the mechanical blunders and the problems in which the pupils failed in part only, an idea of the nature of the errors may be obtained for general purposes by studying them in four general classes:

1. Errors due to a complete absence of thought.
2. Errors in problems correctly performed in principle, but due to lack of reasoning in the processes.
3. Errors due to misinterpretation of a problem.
4. Errors due to lack of knowledge of arithmetical principles.

Of the total number of errors made, the vast majority appear to have been due to a complete absence of thought. Whether in such instances the children did not read the problems carefully, or whether they read them but did not understand them, I am unable to say. What they did was simply to work with the figures, stated or implied, adding, subtracting, multiplying, or dividing at random.

The result of these combinations was called the answer, and the pupils did not stop to consider whether such answers bore any relation whatever to the question. For instance, problem 1, grade 4, reads:

> If there were 4,839 class-rooms in New York City, and 47 children in each class-room, how many children would there be in the New York schools?

The problem did not appear to present much difficulty to the children in any of the schools, and the total number of errors was comparatively small. Nevertheless, nearly 13 per cent of the pupils failed, and of these all but a few divided, giving as their answer $102\frac{45}{47}$ children. It may be reasonably argued that children do funny things; but this does not explain why the number of children who do funny things is so much larger in some schools than in others.

In problem 2, grade 4, three numbers are stated, giving greater scope for variety. The method is, of course, 1,743 + 5,482 = 7,225. 10,000 − 7,225 = 2,775. The varieties presented by the pupils were:

1. 1,743 + 5,482 + 10,000 = 17,225.
2. 5,482 − 1,743 = 3,739. 10,000 − 3,739 = 6,261.
3. 1,743 + 5,482 = 7,225. 7,225 × 10,000 = 72,250,000.
4. 1,743 − 5,482, etc.

The endeavor to subtract a large number from a small one is quite common, and the process in this instance was performed in four ways: (1) By borrowing; (2) by disregarding the thousands; (3) by bringing down the last figure of the upper line; and (4) by bringing down the last figure of the lower line:

1,743	1,743	1,743	1,743
5,482	5,482	5,482	5,482
6,261	2,61	1,261	5,261

On looking over the tables, we find that no particular difficulty was experienced in three of the cities with the first five examples of the 4th grade test; so that the errors may be attributed in some measure to carelessness on the part of pupils who could have done better if they had tried. However, when we direct attention to the results obtained on the remaining three, it becomes apparent that difficulties were here presented which did not occur in the others, and that these difficulties were sufficiently great actually to place the problems beyond the grasp of many of the stronger pupils. On the first five problems the total number of failures was 22 per cent only. But on the sixth example 40 per cent failed, on the seventh, 45 per cent, and on the eighth, nearly 70 per cent.

As the number of failures on the eighth example was large in all the schools represented in the table, the conclusion is justified that it was too difficult for the grade. Examples 1–5 having proved themselves too easy for a test of power, and example 8 too difficult, the actual test was confined to problems 6 and 7. Table 2 shows that the schools represented in the lower two lines did somewhat better than the others on the easiest problems, considerably better on the really difficult one, and much better also on the problems that proved to be the true test of their power. Surely, Cities VI and VII must have been working along the lines of one of these three groups of problems, but they were outranked by the others on all. Under these circumstances, it is difficult to imagine a fourth year test that would reverse the position of the schools, unless it might be purely upon abstract work. But this point is also considered in the tables, where it is shown that Cities VI and VII made not only more errors in reasoning than the others, but also a larger percentage of mechanical errors.

When we consider the nature of problems 6 and 7, it is difficult for the mature mind to see why so many of the pupils should have failed upon them not only in the fourth year, but even in the sixth, *i.e.*, among those who had nearly completed their arithmetic. It will be noticed that problems 6, 7, and 8 were repeated in the test for grades 5 and 6. The questions were:

6. What will 24 quarts of cream cost at $1.20 a gallon?
7. If a boy pays $2.83 for 100 papers, and sells them at 4 cents apiece, how much money does he make?

As to the character of the errors in these problems, the same is true as of the others, namely, that they were thoughtless combinations of the numbers stated. In the sixth, most of the pupils who failed simply multiplied or divided $1.20 by 24, disregarding the

4 entirely; and of those who used it, many multiplied 24 by 4, thus giving 96 gallons as the equivalent of 24 quarts. The typical errors were: $1.20 × 24 = $28.80; $1.20 ÷ 24 = $5; 24 × 4 × 1.20 = $115.20; and 24 ÷ 1.20 = .20.

The difficulty seemed to lie in the fact that the question contained two distinct terms, "quarts" and "gallons," and that a conversion from one into the other was required before proceeding. If the question had been stated in two parts—(1) How many gallons are 24 quarts? and (2) If one gallon of cream costs $1.20, how much will 6 gallons cost?—there is no doubt that most of the children would have performed the example correctly.

In the seventh example the variations in the answers were endless. In this problem, also, two distinct terms are stated, a "hundred" and "apiece," and it is necessary to convert before proceeding. Thus, again, the question would, undoubtedly, have been very well handled if it had been presented in two parts: (1) If a boy sells papers at 4 cents apiece, how much will he get for 100? and (2) If a boy buys 100 papers for $2.83 and sells them for $4, how much money does he make?

The typical errors in this problem were two in number:

$2.83 × 4 = $11.32; and $2.83 ÷ 4 = .70$\frac{3}{4}$.

Among the others the following are interesting: 2.83+4=2.87; 2.83−4=2.79; 2.83 × 4=11.32 ÷ 100=.11; 100 × 4=4.00; 2.83−4.00=.83; 2.83 × 4 = 11.32 ÷ 4 = 2.83. Here the pupil added: "The boy did not make anything."

In a sixth year class, where the pupils had evidently had a thorough drill in decimals, the following remarkable process was found in two instances: $2.83 \div 100 = .283 \times .04 = .01132$. $2.830000 - .01132 = 2.828886$ gain.

Other methods in the same class were:

$283 \times 100 = 28{,}300 + 400 = \$28{,}700$ gain.
$283 \times 100 = 283.00 - 4.00 = \$279.00$.
$283 \div 4 = 70.75$.
$2.83 \times 4 = 11.32 - 1.00 = .32$.
$100 \times 4 = 4.00 \div 2.83 = 1.17 + 100 = 2.17$.

It would be interesting to know what the mathematical ideals in this class really are.

The second class of errors, those occurring in problems worked upon correct principles and due to lack of judgment in performing the various steps, are particularly frequent in problems involving decimals. The errors are here made in the placing of the decimal point, and are due to the fact that, in pointing off, the pupils do not exercise any judgment, but simply trust to luck or their knowledge of the rule. They do not seem to recognize that a blunder in placing the decimal point is liable to make the answer ridiculous, it matters not how carefully the problem may have been performed in every other way.

The first problem in which considerable scope is given for errors of this nature is example 7, grade 5. The correct answer is $1,263; but, by reason of the displacement of the decimal point, many of the pupils obtained $12.63 for the answer. Owing to the nature of the problem, this answer is not on its face ridiculous. It is, however, based on a succession of ridiculous blunders, to wit: 900 barrels of flour at $9 a barrel = $81.00, etc. In the fifth year this error is pardonable, but in the sixth, where the problem is repeated, it should he rare.

While in this particular problem the placing of the decimal point in the wrong position did not produce an absurd answer, the reverse is true of problem 6, grade 6. The question is one in division of decimals, and the answer is this: To obtain 3,896 pounds of salt from salt water containing 8 per cent of salt, it is necessary to evaporate 48,700 pounds of the salt water. Those who saw that it was a problem in division of decimals obtained the figures 48,700 without any difficulty; but the placing of the decimal point where it did not belong made the answer absolutely ridiculous. The answers varied from 48,700 pounds to 4.87 pounds. The statement that it is possible to obtain 3,896 pounds of salt from 487 pounds of salt water was made by a large number of pupils, even in the 7th and 8th grades, where the example was repeated, and not a few said that that amount of salt could be obtained from 4.87 pounds of water.

The ridiculous answers to this problem so late in school life illustrate a weakness in the teaching of arithmetic which seems to be responsible for a large number of blunders in all the grades, namely, the failure to train pupils to see that a problem in arithmetic is a question which calls for a reasonable answer. If the pupils were everywhere trained to scrutinize their answers in the light of the questions, it is probable that many errors of the first class would also be avoided, and that answers stating that the number of children in the New York schools is $102\frac{45}{47}$, and similar absurdities, would be much less frequent than now.

For errors of the second class many teachers are to a certain extent directly responsible, because they believe that a child should receive some credit for a problem if he shows a knowledge of the principles involved. This is, in my opinion, justifiable if a wrong answer should be due to a mechanical error, such as any one is liable to make, in addition, subtraction, multiplication, or division. But I believe that it is an injustice to the child to give him any credit for a problem when, in the light of the question, the answer is absurd.

An interesting phase in the study of errors is found in the problems that are misinterpreted. Errors of this nature very frequently occur in problems in which fractions are involved. For example: Problem 8, grade 5, reads as follows:

> Frank had \$3.08. He spent $\frac{1}{4}$ of it for a cap, $\frac{1}{7}$ of it for a ball, and with the remainder bought a book. How much did the book cost?

Here many of the pupils looked upon $\frac{1}{4}$ and $\frac{1}{7}$ as abstract fractions, not as parts of \$3.08, and worked the problem as follows: $\frac{1}{4}+\frac{1}{7}=\frac{11}{28}$. $308-\frac{11}{28}=307\frac{17}{28}$, cost of the book,

Again, problem 8, grade 6, repeated in grades 7 and 8, reads thus:

A gentleman gave away $\frac{1}{7}$ of the books in his library, lent $\frac{1}{6}$ of the remainder, and sold $\frac{1}{5}$ of what was left. He then had 420 books remaining. How many had he at first?

This problem was treated in many instances in the same way as the one just cited; the fractions being looked upon as purely abstract. The following is an illustration: $\frac{1}{7}+\frac{1}{6}+\frac{1}{5}=\frac{107}{210}$. $420+\frac{107}{210}=420\frac{107}{210}$ books at first. But in this problem a class of errors appeared which I was astonished to find among pupils who had long since completed fractions. It is this, that while, in nearly all instances, the pupils understood the manipulation of fractions, many had no idea of their value. Nearly all were apparently able to add $\frac{1}{7}$, $\frac{1}{6}$, and $\frac{1}{5}$, and get the sum $\frac{107}{210}$. But in adding this fraction to 420, a considerable variety in method was found. Some took the numerator as a whole number, thus: $420+107=527$ books; others so took the denominator: $420+210=630$ books. And some added the denominator to the numerator: $210+107=317$. $420+317=737$ books.

The very low percentages obtained in the seventh and eighth grades of most of the schools examined were due in large part to errors of the fourth class, namely, those arising from a lack of knowledge of the principles involved in the problems. This means nothing more or less than a want of thoroughness in the teaching of the higher grade arithmetic. In some instances, it is true, the pupils did not have the needed insight to see what the problems called for; but in others they did not know how to proceed when they knew what steps were required.

Let us take, for example, problem 4, grade 7:

If coffee sold at 33 cents a pound gives a profit of 10 per cent, what per cent of profit would there be if it were sold at 36 cents a pound?

This problem involves the application of two distinct principles in percentage. The first step lies, of course, in finding the cost, and the second in finding what per cent of 30 is 6, the intermediate step being disregarded. The average obtained on this problem in City VII being only 12.1 per cent, it might be supposed that the principles involved were too difficult for seventh-year pupils to comprehend; but this idea is proved to be erroneous by the fact that in City III, School 1, the average was as high as 96.6.

On looking over the work done upon this example in one of the class-rooms of City VII—a seventh-year class, second half—it was impossible for me to tell what impression the question actually made upon the children. Among the first ten pupils, taking the papers as they came to hand, one only did the first step correctly, and found the cost. The work of some of the others was absolutely meaningless, as the following illustrations will show:

$36 \div 33 = 10\frac{10}{11}$—three cases.

$36 \div 100 = .36$ gain.

$.1000 \div 36 = 27\frac{7}{9}$ profit.

$100 - 36 = 74$. $100 - 33 = 67$. $74 \div 67 = .110$ cost, etc.

It might be argued that the principles of percentage involved are not taught in the seventh grade of all schools, and that the problems would have been more generally suitable for the eighth grade. But this criticism does not help out City VII, because the pupils in the eighth grade of that city made no better showing than those in the seventh on problems based upon similar principles. Problem 6, grade 8, reads:

> Sold steel at $27.60 a ton, with a profit of 15 per cent, and a total profit of $184.50. What quantity was sold?

On this example the average of City VII was 5.1 per cent only, against an average of 88.5 per cent, obtained in City III, School 1.

Among the first ten pupils selected at random, in an eighth-year class, not one understood that it was necessary, in the first place, to find the cost of a ton of steel. Four computed the profit by taking 15 per cent of the selling price; three found the number of tons sold by dividing the selling price per ton by .15; two simply made absurd combinations; and the tenth did not attempt to do the problem.

Having found so much difficulty with the sixth problem, it is not surprising that they failed on the seventh. In that problem, as in the other, not one of the same ten pupils attempted to get at the cost. The profit was given as 20 per cent of the selling price; the loss as 10 per cent of the selling price; and their difference represented the answer.

The data having been presented, it may not be inopportune to inquire, in closing, whether our store of positive knowledge has been in any way enriched by the test. Upon this point opinions differ. A certain number of educators claim that positive knowledge does not come within the scope of pedagogy, and from their standpoint all tests must necessarily be fruitless. On the opposite side, a number of school men may be found who are not only in accord with the method, but believe that at least some of my deductions are conclusive. And, thirdly, there are members of the profession who are heartily in sympathy with the method, but think that more extended investigations are needed before any positive deductions are warranted. While I believe that these people are not altogether right, I also appreciate that they are not entirely wrong. Many of the things I have said or implied may be justly put down as "not proven." But, on the other hand, some of my data point to conclusions so positive that further investigation can neither strengthen nor weaken them. Of these, I shall here mention one only, namely: By reason of the high percentages obtained in certain schools, laboring under ordinary conditions, we must accept as a fact that nearly all children can be trained to solve any ordinary problem in arithmetic, based upon principles they have studied. Consequently, if the normal child is not reasonably proficient in that branch, as far as he has advanced in it, the fault is not his.

Naturally, my explanations as to why some schools succeed and others fail represent merely my personal interpretation of the facts and figures. Others may interpret these differently, and further investigations may upset my explanations. Rome was not built in a day. But as long as it has been positively demonstrated that the child's capacity for arithmetic is considerable, all principals and superintendents should deem it their duty to take steps to learn whether the pupils in their charge are skilled in arithmetic to the extent of their normal capacity, and, if not, to try to discover the reason therefor.

X

THE RESULTS OF A TEST IN LANGUAGE [1]

The test in language on which this article is based was made in April and May, 1903. The examination was undertaken in twenty-two school buildings, representing nine cities, and the total number of children examined was over 8,300. As in arithmetic, so in language, the results have varied enormously, with this difference only, that in language the percentages have run considerably lower. The examination was again given to the pupils of the fourth, fifth, sixth, seventh, and eighth school years, being, in this instance, however, the same for all the grades. The test consisted merely of the reproduction of a story read to the pupils by the teachers.[2] As the work was sprung upon the children without any previous preparation, and the first draft only was accepted, the test was naturally a very severe one; but what was fair for one was fair to all. All the tests whose results I shall publish were, as in arithmetic, taken under my personal supervision. In a few cases the story was sent by request to schools that I did not reach, and the work of the pupils

[1] October-December, 1903.

[2] The story—an account of Pestalozzi's school at Stanz—will be found on page 213.

was forwarded to me; but these schools are not included in the table of results (page 189).

Owing to the courtesy of the school people whom I had the good fortune to approach, the collection of the papers proved to be a comparatively simple affair; but it was not an easy matter for me to decide what to do with the material after it had been snugly deposited in my workshop. The value of my tests depends, of course, upon a trustworthy comparison of the results obtained in different schools, which implies a system of marking that is truly representative of the work of each individual set of papers. In spelling, naturally, the marking is no problem whatever. A word is either right or wrong, and the computing of the class average is a purely mechanical affair. In arithmetic, also, the marking is a comparatively simple matter; although, in that subject, the question of partial credits serves, to a certain extent, to complicate the situation.

Nor is it difficult to work out class averages in language when the test in that branch consists of a series of technical questions, to each of which a certain number of credits is allotted. But my examination was limited to a test of the pupil's ability to express his thoughts in writing, a phase of work that apparently does not permit of marking on a percentage basis—certainly the most intelligible one. But after experimenting for some time in one way and another, there suddenly flashed before my mind a scheme that might make the percentage system feasible; and, to my surprise and gratification, I found, on trial, that it did not only work like a charm, but that it possessed the merit of such remarkable speed that it would give me the opportunity to mark personally, within a reasonable period, every one of the 8,300 papers in my possession; thus insuring a degree of uniformity in criticism that could not have been expected if the papers had been distributed for marking among a number of clerical assistants. In regard to speed, I may mention that I found no difficulty whatever in marking some of the papers at the rate of sixty to seventy an hour.

When I had completed the marking, I began to fear that after all I might have followed a flight of imagination, and that my plan would not stand the test of close inspection. I therefore decided to be on the safe side and go over the work a second time for the purpose of verification. And this I did in the case of all the papers of the sixth, seventh, and eighth school years; but I did not have time to revise the fourth and fifth year marks before the article went to press. As a result of the second marking, the absolute figures were slightly changed, but the relative position of the schools remained practically the same. For this reason, I feel satisfied that the percentages really represent, for all practical purposes, what the work of the respective classes was worth from a comparative point of view.

It might be supposed that in marking for expression, the judgment of the individual examiner would necessarily enter as an important factor. That the personal equation does play a part in the work cannot be denied; but it is no less true that, for our purposes, it is comparatively insignificant. While, in spite of my experience, I could not even now mark a set of papers twice in the same way, nevertheless, this much is certain, that the class average on the two markings would not vary sufficiently to make any material difference. For example, a set of eighth year papers, to make a respectable showing, will have to average not less than 50 per cent. Now, if I should mark an eighth year set and the average should turn out to be 30 per cent, it would be positive proof that the work of that class was poor. If, for the sake of verification, I should then go over the set again, either immediately or at a later period, I might work out a class average of 35 per cent. This, however, would not in any way alter the fact that it was far below the minimum of satisfactory eighth grade work. In a word, I believe that in marking for expression the personal element may be so reduced as to be no greater than it is in marking a set of papers in arithmetic. And the differences in the results in language, as in arithmetic, are so very great that in the present stage of school work the finer distinctions are in no way called for.

As I do not wish any of the above statements to be accepted on faith, I shall, in this chapter, publish a number of carefully selected papers which will not only serve the purpose of demonstrating my system of marking, but which will, at the same time, give the reader at least a little insight into the language work as found in the elementary schools. And as these papers will take up considerable space,

I shall concentrate attention upon them in the present chapter, and defer to the next the discussion of some further details.

As to the plan of marking, it is certainly a very simple one. It lies merely in dividing the papers into five classes—excellent, good, fair, poor, and failure—and marking them on a scale of five; the best papers being given five credits, and the failures one. In changing these figures to percentages, the five's are given 100, the four's 75, the three's 50, the two's 25, and the one's zero. The class averages are then computed in the usual way, by dividing the total number of credits by the number of pupils represented.

The examination having been a test in language, the determining point in the marking was not the thought manifested in the reproduction, but the English—sentence construction, capitalization, punctuation, paragraphing, etc. Naturally, the judgment could not help being biased, to a certain extent, by the construction of the story itself; but, to allay all doubt as to the actual extent to which the story played a part in the marking, I need merely emphasize the fact that the relation between the character of the English and the construction of the story was, as a rule, quite close. That is to say, generally speaking, the pupils who manifested the greatest ability in sentence construction, punctuation, etc., also manifested the greatest ability in the interpretation and reproduction of the story.

I shall now define what I mean by the terms excellent, good, fair, poor, and failure, and then illustrate my definitions by the children's work.

Beginning at the upper end, I may say that the mark 5 was not dispensed with a lavish hand, but was reserved for those papers that were not only, for the most part, accurate in English, but displayed, in addition, an artistic touch. Under these circumstances, it is not surprising that the total number of 5s was not very large. But what is really surprising is the fact that in one set of thirty-four eighth grade papers as many as twelve were 5s, while in each of two other eighth grade sets, containing thirty-five and thirty-seven papers, respectively, as many as ten were 5s. When it is borne in mind that the first draft only was accepted, and that all possibilities of fraud were eliminated by the fact that the papers were collected and carried off by myself before the close of the session, the work of these classes must be looked upon as very remarkable achievements, and altogether beyond what we might expect to find in the elementary schools. A single 5, or even two or three 5s, in a set would not necessarily speak in favor of a school, as a few individual pupils with literary taste might happen to drop into a very ordinary class. But when the work of fully one-third of a class is artistic, that of the next third strong, and the work of the last third passable, I must confess that I am tempted to jump to the conclusion that almost every pupil is capable of acquiring the art of writing good English, and that the normal child is not to blame if he has not acquired the power of expressing his thoughts in creditable English by the time he graduates from the elementary school. And this conclusion is fortified by the fact that I have in my collection no less than five sets of eighth year papers where the work is acceptable almost to the last pupil. In the closing paragraph of my series of articles on arithmetic, I stated that the test had certainly proved this one thing, namely, that every normally constituted child has the ability to acquire a thorough knowledge of arithmetic, and that if he fails to do so the fault is not his; and the same now appears to be true of language.

One of the schools just referred to, and two others, teach us another important lesson. When I had published my results in arithmetic, the opinion was expressed by many that the schools which had made the high percentages in that subject had probably concentrated their attention on arithmetic, and that they would be likely to show lamentable weakness if they should be examined in other branches. I am now in position to say, in answer to this argument, that this theory is not borne out by the facts. Of the eighteen schools examined in arithmetic, six succeeded in obtaining the passing mark, 60 per cent; and of these six schools four were put through my test in language. Now, it so happens that of these four schools three are among the first five of the twenty-two schools examined in language. This would appear to indicate that a successful teacher of arithmetic is also a successful teacher of language. However, the reverse of this does not seem to hold, for some of the schools that were weak in arithmetic did very creditable work in language. Of course, the data that I have collected in regard to this point are too meagre to warrant me in drawing any definite conclusions; but there are certainly indications to the effect that one who has the power to train comparatively dull pupils to see through complicated arithmetical problems has the power to train them thoroughly in other subjects as well.

The papers that I shall now present to illustrate the different types of reproductions, from the 5s down through the 1s, have all been selected from eighth year sets; and, in the marking, I endeavored to adhere to these models, even in the lower grades. Under these circumstances, due allowance will, of course, have to be made for the handicap as we descend from grade to grade; and, basing our expectations on actual achievement, the following standards are not unreasonable: Fourth year, 10 per cent; fifth year, 15; sixth year, 25; seventh year, 37.5; and eighth year, 50. Owing to the very low standards I have set for the fourth and fifth grades, I did not take these classes into account in computing the average for each school as a whole, but based the latter on the work of the sixth, seventh, and eighth school years. Thus, the passing average of a school has been placed at 37.5; and a glance at Table I will show that, of the twenty-two buildings examined, seven only succeeded in meeting this demand—just the same proportion as in arithmetic.

As the above figures do not convey the same meaning as do percentages in spelling or arithmetic, because we are not here dealing with the method of right and wrong cases, it might be well to call the reader's attention to the following. Speaking in a general way, a set of papers that averages 25 per cent is composed mainly of papers marked 2 and contains a 3 for every 1. A set that averages 37.5 is composed principally of 2s and 3s and contains a 4 for every 1. A set that averages 50 is composed chiefly of 3s and contains a 4 for every 2. And a set whose percentage is 75 is made up mainly of 4s and contains a 5 for every 3. With the aid of these formulæ and the typical illustrations, the reader may form a fairly accurate idea of the character of a set of papers of any given percentage.

The following are a few illustrations of the type of reproductions marked 5:

About a hundred years ago, in far off Switzerland, there existed the little hamlet of Stanz in which were many poor people. A dreadful war had made homeless a score of little children, and it was to provide for these orphans that a school was originated. Unlike the modern ones of to-day was that little school. It consisted of one room in an old, ruined convent. But it was the best and only place the town afforded. Its master, a kind old man and a lover of children, had their interests at heart and desired to make good men of the boys, even though poverty so early retarded their progress. He found it difficult to teach the children at first, but after they discovered his feeling toward them, they did their utmost to please him. Owing to the limited space, all their time was spent in the one room. There they ate, slept, and had their lessons, for the teacher had generously undertaken to keep house for them as well as instruct them. He was constantly with them and acted as their companion, even taking part in their sports. As an amusement, he frequently told them stories after lessons were over.

But it was not their privilege to remain here long. War,

TABLE I

	School.	4			5			6			7			8			School average—6, 7, and 8 grades.	Minutes daily—oral.	Minutes daily—written.	Total minutes daily.	Per cent pupils American parentage.
		Number of pupils.	Average age.	Class average.	Number of pupils.	Average age.	Class average.	Number of pupils.	Average age.	Class average.	Number of pupils.	Average age.	Class average.	Number of pupils.	Average age.	Class average.					
City I	1	30	....	12.5	80	12.0	23.7	70	13.5	36.8	37	14.2	46.5	25	14.6	70.0	51.1	30	7	37	81
City II	1	148	12.1	9.9	133	12.6	13.1	88	13.4	33.8	59	14.0	42.9	34	14.9	76.2	50.9	30	10	40	71
City II	2	68	11.8	10.6	127	12.7	20.9	132	13.9	25.4	113	14.1	38.8	71	15.4	73.8	46.0	25	25	50	83
City III	1	188	....	13.4	150	12.2	17.7	124	13.4	31.8	74	13.9	49.4	47	14.8	56.6	45.9	28	20	48	28
City IV	1	111	11.6	14.3	114	12.3	22.2	99	12.9	35.4	65	13.6	43.4	73	14.7	56.0	44.9	24	13	37	74
City V	1	40	11.0	15.5	100	11.8	16.0	74	12.9	31.2	73	13.9	44.5	49	14.4	51.7	42.4	29	18	47	85
City II	3	....	....	....	121	...	22.5	107	....	28.7	96	....	34.8	92	....	56.0	39.8	..	..	.	..
City II	4	69	11.7	6.5	82	12.8	7.0	57	12.8	26.8	43	13.8	29.7	60	14.9	51.1	35 8	27	22	49	64
City II	5	121	11.4	5.6	189	12.4	15.7	81	13.1	23.3	48	13.4	39.2	45	14.5	41.7	34.7	19	14	33	6
City I	2	82	11.7	11.5	69	12.6	14.8	36	13.2	30.5	29	14.2	25.7	43	14.9	40.5	32.2	42	8	50	74
City V	2	75	10.9	2.5	61	11.9	8.7	72	12.6	19.9	39	13.7	23.8	46	14.3	53.2	32.1	18	18	36	56
City V	3	75	10.8	7.5	163	11.7	5.1	176	12.7	19.5	66	13.8	24.4	71	14.6	46.6	30.2	15	17	32	75
City V	4	89	...	0	08	11.8	5.2	04	12.7	15.4	82	13.4	29.8	40	14.7	42.5	29.2	..	..	..	15
City VI	1	23	11.0	0	51	11.0	4.8	33	12.5	26.8	31	13.8	23.2	36	14.4	35.0	28.3	30	10	40	85
City III	2	119	....	2.0	186	12.2	6.8	124	12.8	21.2	95	13.9	25.1	76	15.0	35.6	27.3	20	10	30	71
City VII	1	112	10.6	2.8	80	11.3	9.1	79	12.3	16.5	139	13.3	18.0	61	14.2	45.7	26.7	30	12	42	71
City III	3	82	11.1	1.7	82	12.2	9.5	71	12.7	14.8	37	13.5	26.5	40	14.1	36.5	25 9	54	18	72	34
City VIII	1	37	11.7	6.0	88	12.3	7.7	78	13.2	12.2	57	13.9	27.0	44	14.5	38.7	25.9	30	8	38	64
City IV	2	129	11.5	5.6	84	11.8	13.7	64	12.8	16.7	37	13.8	24.2	27	14.7	35.5	25.4	35	14	49	58
City IX	1	59	10.2	5.7	66	11.0	11.6	67	12.5	16.1	55	13.2	26.1	53	14.3	32.0	24.7	36	11	47	67
City IX	2	30	11.0	4.5	66	11.6	7.8	64	12.6	12.7	51	13.5	21.0	34	14.3	29.6	21.1	25	7	32	43
City VII	2	116	....	0	73	11.6	5.7	121	12.3	15.5	106	13.0	15.7	72	14.1	29.4	19.1	33	18	51	37
General average	..	....	....	6 8	....	....	12.2	...	....	23.2	....	....	30.6	....	....	47.0					
Number of pupils	..	1,802	....	....	2,163	......	....	1,821	....	....	1,433	....	....	1,138	....	....	Total, 8,357.				

the bane of their existence as it seemed, again broke out, and one day, about a year after they had entered the school, a battle was fought near Stanz. Wounded soldiers were carried into the village to be cared for, and as no place for their shelter, other than the room in the convent, was available, a man was sent to inform the master of the sorrowful fact that the school must be given up. Sadly and reluctantly, the boys prepared to leave the building, old and dilapidated though it was, where they had spent the happiest and brightest days of their lives, and around which in after years they were to associate many pleasant memories.

Very soon after the close of the bloody war with Austria, Stanz, a poor Swiss village which had suffered heavily in the campaigns near it, established a home and school for the orphan sons of the sacrificed soldiers. It was a humble room in a poor convent, but in it the boys ate, slept, and studied. They were cared for and instructed in their lessons by an old man who was fond of children, and so volunteered to act as their father and teacher. At first the boys, unaccustomed to anything but entire liberty, disliked him, but soon, as they realized and appreciated the sacrifice he was making for them, they joined to love and praise him.

They were not destined, however, long to remain in this haven of safety, for, within a year of its foundation, war again broke out. Again a battle was fought near Stanz, and many Swiss were wounded. The school-room was the only place available for their protection, and the boys were for the time deprived of their home.

About a hundred years ago, there existed in a little town of Switzerland, named Stanz, a school, which was made for the purpose of educating some poor boys. The parents of these children were killed in a war, leaving their children orphans and destitute of food and shelter.

The school consisted of but one room in an old convent. It was poorly provided for, but the people of Stanz were not wealthy and could do only a little for such a cause. The charge of this little school was given to an old man who was kind and thoughtful and very fond of children. Because this one room was all they had, it had to serve for every purpose. Here they ate, studied and slept, but their devoted teacher was so kind to them in every way, they were glad to endure some hardships.

There was one obstacle, however. At that time children were not made to attend school, and because of this many did not study, and remained uneducated. So it was with these boys. They felt that the master asked too much of them when he forced them to study and learn. But he talked with them kindly and coaxed them to be studious. Soon they discovered that all he did was for their own good, that when they studied and learned it was for their own benefit and theirs only. Then they were anxious to learn. They wanted to be good and noble men, to learn what their master would teach them and be well educated.

Only a year had this little school room been in use when a war broke out in the neighborhood of Stanz. One day a battle was fought near by and several wounded soldiers were brought into the town for shelter. Unfortunately the officer who was in charge of them could find no place to put them, and after a while he found a room in an old convent which would answer his purpose. This room was our little school room, and solemnly the officer told the old master what was his wish. The master consented, and the boys had to leave their old devoted companion who had cared for them, taught them, and played with them, to enter the world alone. They did so sorrowfully, but their master had taught them to care for themselves and be brave, honest lads.

The reproduction of the type marked 4 differs from the 5 in that it is altogether lacking in that originality which lends to the latter its artistic flavor. Its characteristic features are: (1) That it is composed of well-constructed sentences; (2) that it is nearly or quite free from technical errors; and (3) that it relates a well-defined, connected story. A set that starts out with a 4 and maintains that standard to the middle of the class makes a very favorable impression, and is highly satisfactory.

One of the eighth year sets in my possession is composed almost entirely of 4s, and, from the standpoint of uniform excellence, is a remarkable demonstration of the fact, above referred to, that by means of thorough instruction even the dullest pupils can be trained to write good English. The following are examples of 4s:

About a hundred years ago, there existed in the city of Stanz, in Switzerland, a school for poor boys.

Before this time a terrible war had broken out and a great many children were left orphans, so an old man offered to take care of them. A small room in a convent was given to them, and it was used as their school-room, bed-room, and their living-room.

At first the little children did not like the old man, because he made them work, but after they found out that what he was doing was for their own benefit, they began to love and obey him. He not only taught them, but also entered into their games, often amusing them with funny stories.

As you may think these little ones loved their home, but they were not allowed to remain in it long. Another war broke out and a battle was fought near Stanz, the captain found out that the only place of shelter for the wounded soldiers was this little room in the convent. The captain told the old man of it, and the poor motherless little ones were turned out of their home, which they loved so much.

About one hundred years ago in the little town of Stanz, in Switzerland, there was a school for poor orphan boys.

The school itself was not large and was situated in one room of an old convent. The keeper of the school was a kind old man who was fond of children. When the school was started he offered to keep the little ones and also teach the others. The school was very poor but the people around the school were very poor too and it was the best they could give these poor orphans, whose mothers and fathers had been killed during a great war.

The children at this time were not obliged to go to school

and the schoolmaster found it very hard to make them learn.

At first the children did not like him because he made them learn, but when they found out it was for their own good they began to love and obey him.

As this one room was all that was given them it was used for everything and in this room they ate, slept and went to school.

Unfourtuneatly they only went to school one year when another war broke out. One day there was a battle near Stanz and several of the soldiers were wounded and it was found there was only one place to take them and was in the little school room.

The officer then came to the old schoolmaster and told him what he needed and so the little school room in the old convent was turned into a hospital. So the children were forced to leave the little school they had learned to love so well.

When we come to the papers marked 3, we arrive at the point where the complications begin to set in. The typical 5s and the typical 4s are very plain sailing, as they are practically unmistakable; but the 3s are of different types, which may, however, be divided into two classes. Of these, one class is practically unmistakable; but the other calls for the exercise of judgment, and some examiners might be disposed to mark the papers of this class 4.

The unmistakable 3 is a reproduction that resembles the typical 4, both in the sentence construction and in the construction of the story, but differs from it in that it contains a number of very palpable flaws, such as poorly constructed or incomplete sentences, errors in expression or verbal forms, the occasional running of sentences together, etc. Nevertheless, in form and structure, papers of this type contain enough good points to save them from being classed as poor. The papers belonging to the other class of 3s are practically free from actual errors, but present the one characteristic feature of weakness, which, in my opinion, makes them unworthy of being classed with the 4s. The following are illustrations of papers marked 3:

About one hundred years ago in the city of Stanz Switzerland a school for poor boys was started. This school was for the boys who had lost their parents in the terrible struggle just before this time. The school comprised only one room, this was for the pupils to live in and to have school.

This school was not a very comfortable one it was in an old covent. Their teacher was an old man who loved children very much. At first the pupils did not like their teacher, (but) because he made them work and learn their lessons. In those days the children were not sent to school and this was the reason why they were not willing to study and learn.

The people of Stanz were poor, and they could not afford a better school. At last the children began to love their teacher, he was always with them and tried to make every pleasant for them. He took part in their games and sports and sometimes would tell him interesting stories.

The school did not last for more than a year when one day the war broke out again and battle was fought near Stanz, and some soldiers were wounded. the officer went Stanz to find a place for the wounded soldier but he could not find one in the city except the one room in the covent. The officer went to the school and told the master his story. The teacher gave him the school for the soldiers and the boys had to leave their home they loved so well.

About one hundred years ago in a small town called Stanz, in Switzerland their were a great many poor boys whose fathers had been killed in war. In this town their lived a very kind old man who agreed to teach and take care of these poor boys.

The only place they could find for a school-room was a small room in a convent.

At first the boys did not like their school-master because

he made them work, but they soon leared it was for their good that he was doing it and they loved and obeyed him.

But these poor boys did not have much room for they had to study, eat and sleep in this one little room. These boys did not keep their abode long, for one day (about a year after they had been—there—there was a battle near Stanz and a great many soldiers were wounded, and the General came to Stanz to see if he could find a shelter for these poor wounded soldiers, and the only place he could find was the boys school-room so he mournfully came to the schoolmaster and asked him if he would let him shelter the soldier there & the school-master said yes & so the poor boys were turned on the street again.

As we continue on our downward path the complications increase, and by the time we get into the middle of the 2s the papers begin to lose a well-defined form. The reproductions of class 2 are manifestly poor; and their distinguishing feature is that the flaws outweigh the good points, while there is still enough of the righteous in them to save them from being classed as actual failures.

At the upper end of the 2s, *i.e.*, at the line of demarcation between them and the 3s, we still find papers whose structure resembles that of the 4s; but they abound in errors of one kind or another, and are therefore not difficult to distinguish. An example follows:

About a hundred years ago their was a terrible war broke out near "Stanz" in Switzerland. Their was quite a good many boys who lost their parnets and lost their home. The people of Stanz were poor but they tried to help these boys. They found out for them an old convent. This convent had but one room in it. An old man said that he would go & live with these boys & be their master.

The boys at first did not like him, because he tried to teach them but they soon liked him for trying to teach them. He was very kind to them & did all he could to help them & he soon made them happy & they did not think so much of their dear father & mother who were gone of them.

This kind old man did not only teach them but also entered into some of their games. He often told them stories. He was like a companion to them he was always with them.

As I said their was one room in the convent they had to —sleep—eat their meals & also to learn their lessons & play their games here sometimes. These boys did not hate their school master any more but loved him, dearly.

About a year after they had lived in this convent another war broke out near by & their were many soldiers who were injured. The commander of these soldiers (who were hurt) wanted a place to take them. The poor people of Stanz did not know of any place that he could take them at last he found out this place where the boys had lived with their schoolmaster for about a year so peaceably with one another.

He came to the master of these poor boys & told him that their was a good many soldiers who had been hurt in this out break of war & he said he had not place to take them. So the master said that he could have the convent which only had the one room in it & the boys gave up their home to the sick & injured soldiers.

This was turned into a hospital for the soldiers. The boys love this convent but gave it up to the sick.

Next we find papers that have but little in their favor beyond properly constructed sentences sandwiched between faulty ones:

About a hundred years, in Switzerland a place called Stanz their was opened a school in a convent. The people in Stanz were poor themselves and could not pay much to support the school. The school consisted of one room occupied by orphans who had lost their parents during a terrible, in this room they had school, ate there lunch, played, also slept. The place was taken care of by an old man who was the boys teacher. They did not like him very much because he made them learn and boys in Stanz were not compelled to go to school, but when they seen he was teaching them and doing everything for there own good they began to like this old man. He played with them in all there games and was just like a brother to them.

But a war had broke out again and one day a battle took place near Stanz and some soldiers were wounded and the only place the captain could find to put the wounded soldiers was in the school room in the convent, thus the poor boys had to leave there school room just as they were beginning to love it.

I have also classed among the 2s the papers of pupils who are able to construct fairly good sentences, but who are in the habit of repeatedly running them together.

Of the 1s it is not necessary to say a great deal, as they speak so eloquently for themselves, and represent merely an infinite variety of examples of English as it should *not* be written. On considering papers of this nature, the uninitiated will be likely to conclude that their authors, by reason of unfavorable hereditary influences, had entered this mundane sphere with brains incapable of normal development, or, by reason of unfavorable home environment, had had their intellects stunted during the pre-scholastic period. But my dear reader of the uninitiated class, I beg of you not to believe anything of the kind, but to take my word for it that in the vast majority of such cases the pre-scholastic period was innocent.

As, in most instances, the percentages in the fourth and fifth year classes were very low, it is evident that the test was too severe for these grades. Indeed, all things considered, 60 per cent of failures in the fourth year, and 40 per cent in the fifth, may be looked upon as pardonable. However, already in the sixth year some comparatively good work was done; and, judging by the general results, an allowance here of 33 per cent of failures is liberal. In the seventh grade, the failures should not have exceeded 20 per cent, and in the eighth they should have been reduced to 5 per cent. I have, indeed, in my possession at least half a dozen eighth year sets that are absolutely free from failures. Nevertheless, some of the sixth year sets were composed almost entirely of 1s; some of the seventh year sets contained as many as 60 per cent of them; while several eighth year sets contained 30 per cent or over, one of them running as high as 42.

The following are illustrations of papers of this type:

About one hundred years ago in the city of Stanz in Switzerland there was a home statarted for poor boys and this school was conducted by and old man who taught them and played with them, most of these children were orphans and this school was started principally for them, it was one room where they ate there meals and slept, after they had been in the school for about one year the war broke out again and there was a battle fought near Stanz and there was a number of soldiers wounded and there was know place to put the wounded soldiers so the Commander of the army came to see the teach to tell him he would like to have the room for the wounded Soldiers and the little school was broken up and the little children had to give up there homes.

About a hundred year ago there was a school started for poor boy, the school was in Stanz Switzerland. The school was for the boy who parents were killed in a terrible war. The school was not neat or comfortable, it was in an old room of an convent, they had a kind teacher, who cooked for them and did every thing he could for them.

In Stanz the boys were not compelled to go to school, so the teacher had a hard time in getting his pupils togeather. The boy thought he was a cross teacher because he made them work, but it was for their own good, soon the boy found that he was kind to them, he used to be with them in all their games and to amuse then he tell them stories.

In the room where they had the school was not only a school room, but the boy sleept and eat and have school in the one room. This was the best school the people in Stanz could afford because they were poor themselves.

This school did not last long. In about a year a war broke out near Stanz, and several soilders were wounded. The injures were carried in to town who were care for by an officer, they looked all over for shelter but could not find it, at last the Officer came to the school room and he was very sad, he told the school teacher that they would have to give up the school for shelter for the wounded soldiers, so the school was turned into a hospital.

The boy had to leave their good home and go seeking for another.

About one hundred years ago there resisted in Stanzs in switzerland a school for poor boy who had no father and mother. This school was kept purpose for making homes for the poor boys.

The place where this school was kept was neither large or comfortable. It consisted of one large room and home. A very kind old man promised to be their teacher and also their house keeper and the little ones althought the boys did not like him at first because he made them work; but when they saw it was for their good they loved him. He taught them and played games and even told storys. But they did not stay this way long for a terrible war broke out and a battle was fought near Stanzs.

The wounded soldiers were brought to the village and the only place for them were in this school. The poor boys gave up the school they love.

In addition to 1s of the foregoing types, I have

come across a great many papers that are, strictly speaking, even below zero; and, as they make rather interesting reading, it may not be out of place to publish a few of them here. However, while they all appear to be literary curiosities, I wish to direct attention to the fact that papers such as the following, all taken from fourth year sets, do not represent isolated cases, but are more or less representative of the work of lower classes whose averages did not exceed 5 or 6 per cent.

About one hundred years ago a boy broke, out many poor boy lost his home.
And a old man said I will be the teacher and mind the house.
This person was killed in the war.
The school only had one room,
And they never liked their teacher, because they made it to a hospital, and the poor boys loved their teacher.

About 1600 year ago it was home for Poor boy.

It was kept at the Stanz in Switzerland.

A man was the teacher, and kept the milps to give the poor boy to eat.

They thought that the man is giveing to hard work. But the man said it was for thier own stake.

After they were sheltred in war they broke open the home and maid a hostipal.

The man learn them game and read book for them to make them happier.

They stoud one year in the little home.

"I am going to say a story and I am going to," asked you one.

A hundred years ago children lost their parents in the Stanz Switzerland. They were poor and had no home. They went to school where they could sleep, and an old man used to teach them to read. The children did not like to stay in the school, but they gave them a room where they sleep, school and meal and sheletered themselves. Afterward they went to a house called the hospels, and the poor children did not like to stay in one room, but the man teach then to read, write and sing. Afterward the children became happener and were friend.

A school for poor boy's About a hundred years ago there was a war where many people got killed in war And a man bluit a school for poor boy's and many people got killed and some boy's never had a mother or a father and so they went to school and after a boy told the man in school that it ought to go to a hosipel and so they all left school and they thanket the man for the school."

I am going to tell a story about one of our own.

About two hundred years ago in Stanza Switzerland there was a school room. It was large and comfortable. There was a terrible war and the teacher had trouble teaching them. A man who was fond of children one day he said there were two orphans. About a year there was a terrible war. They called many wounds soldiers and it was a war.

The school became a very large hosiptal and children lost their parents by war. A man consist of a great many folks and they companion. They had a oparns house and they thought it was there home. The childrens afterwards were glad and had no trouble more.

There were poor boys which they have lost their parents and they go to a small school in Switzerland. So they eat dirnk and slept and even the teacher eat, drank and slept. Nearly two hundrend years ago there was a small school in Switzerland and that school was for poor boy's. And it told the whole room to write a story about a schol for poor boy's and it told us to write it with ink and write it neat. At first they didn't like to go to school then he thought them something in school. And then they liked school and they had to stay with the teacher.

About one hundred years ago there was a Stanz in Switzerland and there were a lot of poor boy in that Stanz that had no parents they went to war and the poor children had to go to that Stanz and that stanz was made into every thing

And the man who had charge of it was a very nice man he use to play with them and the teacher had hard work to get the boy's in to learn

And they did not like him and after a time their heard that is was for their good so the work for him and obeyed him

So not long after their was a war broke out and waght near the stanz and the officer of their army said I know only one place and that was the Stanz was made into a hospital and wounded soldiers was in there and the boor children hard to leave their home wich they like it very well. it was all occant of the soldier their had to leave there home

---

After one hundred year ago there is in Switzerland a little school for poor boys. It was put on for purpose until the dureful war. It was meater large or comfortable. For the boys how had lost their plarnes in the dreadful war. It was keep by an old man in a room connection. First they did not like him because he made them work and he learned them how to play games and tell stories and them they love him. Then another war broke out an a number of soldiers were brang in the room connectent. The officers that were in the war brang this soldiers and then it was made a hosipal, and the children would not stay no longer.

Nearly 100 year ago in town of Stanz on Switzerland there ofen a little school for the poor boys that they last they parent with a trowble war. And they us to go the school every day and they had they neatl in the little roon of the house school. But often a while they love they master and they obley in and then became to made a battle and they had a big war of soldiers that the school had to be change into hospital that the little poor boys had to do the little home for they self.

I am goning to Read you a stor hunded yeaer a gon.

Thay was in Stanz was waler and the chelden pares got celt in the waler and they din have now school to gon to and after thay was lettle school open? And it was one room the school and thay take the meyls in the same room in Switzerland and the chelden den like the teacher but after thay fan out that. He was doing it for ther sak the chelden began the like him He was gan hope then in the gam and ever thing that He cund do? Not a yaer after a nother waler brok out ner biy in Switzerland. And then thay was wonded solid thay was onty one plays to breing them to the old convet school and then it was twon to and horsepoilt and then the chelden was tuon out of ther home? And the solid was in it?

Having illustrated my system of marking, I shall now direct the reader's attention to the results, which are given in Table I. A glance at that table will show that in the fourth year the grade averages have varied between 15.5 per cent and zero; in the fifth year, between 23.7 and 5.1; in the sixth, between 36.8 and 12.7; in the seventh, between 46.5 and 15.7; and in the eighth, between 76.2 and 29.4. Taking the figures just as they stand, we find that the best fourth year work was as good as the poorest seventh, and the best fifth year work not far below the poorest eighth.

But the percentages given in the table tell less than the whole truth, because they merely represent the work of a grade as a whole, while in most schools each grade is composed of several individual classes, sometimes as many as five. Taking the averages of individual classes, we naturally find the extreme variations to be still greater. Fourth grade, 22.5 to zero; fifth grade, 35.0 to 2.0; sixth grade, 46.2 to 5; seventh grade, 52.2 to 8.5; and eighth grade, 76.2 to 19.0. When the figures are examined from this narrower point of view, we see that the best fourth year work was better than the poorest eighth.

But, taking a very broad survey, and comparing the averages obtained in all the grades of the first six schools in Table I with those obtained in all the grades of the last six, *i.e.*, comparing the schools comprising the first quarter of the table with those comprising the last quarter, we find a difference in favor of the former of almost two school years. The figures follow (Table II):

TABLE II.

Grade	4.	5.	6.	7.	8.
6 highest	12.7	18.9	32.4	44.2	64.0
6 lowest	3.9	9.3	14.6	23.4	33.6

The results given in Table II are the more remarkable in that, comparatively speaking, they show the conditions in language to be almost identical with those that were found in arithmetic, where the highest six schools of the eighteen examined were two school years ahead of the lowest five. In view of the fact that recent educational discussion has dealt so largely with plans and methods of shortening the course of training from the elementary school up through the university, the lesson taught by my tests in arithmetic and language should not be entirely overlooked.

The figures are certainly striking, and the conclusion to be drawn from Table II cannot be doubted except on the ground that my system of marking had not been carefully applied in practice. That the system may be misapplied I do not hesitate to admit. The difficulty does not lie with the typical cases, which are distinctive enough, but with the papers that lie so close to the border line between 4 and 3, or 3 and 2, etc., that it is not easy to decide whether to give them the higher or the lower mark. What I have endeavored to do in such instances has been to remain on the safe side by marking the strong sets hypercritically and giving the weaker ones the benefit of the doubt.

However that may be, to allay all doubt, even after the second marking had been completed, I decided to subject the whole system to a test which would be conclusive. This test lay in taking in hand certain individual sets of different degrees of excellence, as shown by the class averages, and arranging the papers in such a way that they would follow each other in the order of merit, from the first to the last. This arrangement then gave me an opportunity to compare the individual papers of sets having high percentages with those of sets having low percentages. The method was an extremely laborious one, but the effort was well repaid, as it really served to dispel all doubt. For an accurate comparison of two sets of papers by this method, it is necessary to compare the papers of different parts of these sets, on a scale down; but, for general purposes, the middle one is fairly representative.

To give the reader an opportunity to judge matters for himself, I shall now place before him ten papers, the middle one of a strong and a weak set, respectively, of each of the grades from the fourth to the eighth. Moreover, this will give him an opportunity not only to note the marked difference between strong and weak work in each individual grade, but to compare the strong work of a lower grade with the weak work of a higher one. The latter form of comparison will show that the work of a strong fifth grade was unquestionably superior to that of a weak eighth. As to the contest between the strong fourth and the weak eighth, I cannot see that there has been a decided victory on either side. However, if the former should be given just a little leeway, and the second paper above the middle one of the fourth grade compared with the second below the middle one of the eighth year set, the former would win by a respectable margin, as the reader will see.[1]

To avoid needless complications, I have selected all the poor papers in the following exhibit from schools whose pupils enjoy home surroundings at least as favorable as those enjoyed by the pupils of the school that stands second in Table I.

Middle paper from a fourth year class averaging 22.5 per cent:

A number of years ago there was a great many boys who had no parents, there parents were killed in a war.

There was an old man who took care of these children, he

[1] In order to guard against the possibility of going astray in this particular instance, I requested a number of superintendents to meet at my office for the purpose of looking over the two sets that I had selected as the poorest eighth and the best fourth grade work. To my surprise, the verdict was unanimous to the effect that I had erred on the conservative side, because they all agreed that the fourth year set was better than the eighth.

had a small school where they were taught many lessons, they lived, ate, and slept there.

These children were very poor but they did not seem to mind that much.

The school was a very small, and uncomfortable school, it had but one room in it.

After about a year another war broak out. this war was near Stanz. Stanz is in Switzerland. This small school was in Stanz.

The war was a sad war and many people were killed and hurt.

The children had to leave the school and it was made a hospital for the people who were hurt in the war.

Middle paper from a fourth year class averaging 6.0 per cent:

Long ago there was a school for poor boys who parents were dead in the time of a terble war in Stanz in Switzerland ladies go and can mot come out again.
There was a war near Stanz city and the soilder had to come here to stay in was the only place they could go to.
The teacher was an old man how loved children and at first the children hated hin because he made them work. but a while after they begun to love him.
There was only one room in this hospital and they had to study and eat there meal, and sleep to. the children had mo home they had to give up there loved school.

Middle paper from a fifth year class averaging 35.0 per cent:

About one hundred years ago in the little town of Stanz in Switzerland, a school was founded for some poor boys, they were orphans for their parents had been killed in great war which had taken place a long time before. The school consisted of one room in an old Convent, in which they slept, ate, and studied. Their teacher was a kind old man and offered to keep house for them as well as teach them, but at first the boys did not like him for he made them study, and in those days boys were not compelled to go to school. But when they found out that he was doing it for their own good they began to love him, he not only helped them with their studies, but joined in their games and told them stories.

One day a war brok out and a battle was fought near Stanz, many soldiers were wounded, and the only shelter they could get was in the room in the old Convent where the boys lived. When the Captian told the teacher, the teacher turned the school room into a hospital and the boys had to leave the home they had learned to love so well.

Middle paper from a fifth year class averaging 10.0 per cent:

About a hundred years ago there lived a little boy in Stanz of Switzerland he had lost his parents and he went to a little house where lots of other poor children were to.

There was an old man who loved children and he would teach them. At first the children did not like the man, but after a while they began to like him better.

After they had finished this work they would go out and play and some times the man would play with them to.

The old house was a convent and it was used by the poor boys as a school, eating and sleeping all in the same room.

One day a was broke out near Stanz and some of the men were wounded, and that house was the only place the soldiers could get shelter. so the oficer took the men there and now it was used for a hospitle, and the poor boys had to seek shelter for them selfs.

Middle paper from a sixth year set averaging 41.5 per cent:

About a hundred years ago there was a school started in the city of Stanz in Switzerland. It was for boys whose parents had been killed in the war.

There was a man who was their teacher and their house-keeper. They had only one room and in that they slept, studied and ate their meals. He was their companion and was always with them he not only helped them with their tasks but joined them in their plays and told them stories.

At first he had hard work to get very many scholars as children were not made to go to school in those days.

They hadn't been in the school but about a year when another war broke out. The captain wanted some place to put the wounded soldiers and he couldn't find any place but the schoolhouse. He was very sorry but he kindly asked the school-teacher if he could have it and so they had to give it up so they could use it for a hospital.

Middle paper from a sixth year set averaging 17.0 per cent:

About a hundred years ago in a little town in Switzerland called Stanz there were a lot of boys who's parents had [did] died in a terrible war.

The people of Stanz were poor so they could not give these boys a home finally the thought they could send them to an old comvent for a school.

This school was neither large or comfortable, they had a single room in this the ate stuided and slept.

They were placed in charge of a kind old man who loved children, he said he would keep house for them, so the children were sent here to school.

But they had hardly been there a year when war broke out again and a battle was fought near Stanz and a lot of wounded soldiers were brought into stanz, the officer in charge found that the only place they could be brought was this school room so the boys were oblidged to give up the home they had learned to love so well.

Middle paper from a seventh year set averaging 45.0 per cent:

About one hundred years ago there was an old schoolhouse in a convent in Stanz, Switzerland. In this schoolhouse there was only one room, it was given as a schoolroom, sleeping-room and lunchroom for poor boys whose parents were killed during war. There was an old man who was very fond of children, and took the place as teacher and companion.

At this time they were not compelled to go to school, and it was very hard to make them study.

When they were in not quite a year war broke out, and as there was no other place for the wounded soldiers the schoolhouse was given to them, but the officer asked the teacher in a very kind manner, and the children had to give up their home they loved so well.

So out of this old schoolhouse, there was a home for the wounded and dying soldiers.

Middle paper from a seventh year set averaging 19.1 per cent:

Once upon a time about one hundred years ago there was a war near a city named Stany, Switzerland. All the people when war broke out enlisted. After the war many fathers and mothers were killed and there were a large number of orphans.

So the city gave the a convent were they could go to school and learn. It was give to a good kind-hearted old man who was very fond of children.

It was not a very comfortable place. But it had to do because the people were not very rich.

After it was started and the schoolmaster put them to work they began to dislike him. But after they found out that he was doing it for their good they began to like him.

In those days boys and girls do not go to school but work. So it was hard for the school-master to get them to work.

In this schoolhouse the children cooked, selpt, and study all in the same room.

After a while a war broke out near Stanz and a number of soldiers were killed and wounded. But . those who were wounded had no place to go but to go to this little school house in Stanz. So this little convent was made in a hospital.

Middle paper from an eighth year set averaging 75.0 per cent:

About a hundred years ago there existed in Stanz, a town in Switzerland, a little school. This school was provided for a number of poor boys, who had lost their fathers in a terrible war. The only place that could be found for this purpose, was a room in an old convent. It was neither large nor comfortable as the people in Stanz were very poor, but it was the only refuge that could be had for the poor orphans.

There was a kind old man, who was very fond of children and he offered to keep house and also teach the boys. As the children were not obliged to go to school in those days, the old man had a great deal of trouble to teach them. But he was very patient with them, and entered into their games, so, in a short time they grew to love the old man and tried to learn their lessons, as they found it was for their own good.

If we think of having school, eating our meals and sleeping in one room we must certainly think of these little boys as heroes. The school had not been kept a year yet, when another war broke out. There was a battle fought near Stanz and a number of wounded soldiers were brought into the town. The officer in charge could find no place of shelter for them, but the little school and sadly told the old man that it would have to be turned into a hospital; and the little orphans were forced to leave the school they had learned to love so well.

Middle paper from an eighth year set averaging 22.2 per cent:

About one hundred years ago in the little town of Stanz in Switzerland there lived a good many children who's fathers were killed in a war. In this town of Stanz there lived a man, (he was an old man) he said that he would take these children and teach them. As all the other people were poor he had to take them to an old Convent where they had but one room in which to eat, sleep, and have their school.

The old man not only taught them but played in their games with them. But as the children did not have to go to school in those days the children of this school did not like the man becaus he said that they all had to do as he said but after a time they understood that it was for their own good and so they got to like him.

But the school was not to last long becaus there was another war that broke out and one battle was fought near Stanz and when it was over the wounded soldiers were taken into Stanz and when it was found that there was no place but one to put them the children lost their schooling. Becaus the only place to make a hauspittle was the one little room in the Convent wher the children had their school.

Two above middle paper of fourth year set averaging 22.5 per cent:

About 100 years ago there existed a small school for orphan's whose parents were kill in war. The school consisted of one room in the Convent. It was not very comforttabel. This school was in Stanz a city in Switzerland.

An old kind man took care of these children and was thier school master. At first the children did not like there master becase he made work. But after awhile they began to see how much good it did to them.

But the children did not stay even a year. Another war broke out near Stanz. The capten brought some wounded soldiers to Stanz. The only place he could keep them in, was the school in the convent. The poor boys never knew how they liked home and master till they had to leave the home. The captain came to the old man and asked if he could have the school. So the school was turned into a Hospital for the wounded Soldiers.

Two below middle paper of eighth year set averaging 22.2 per cent:

About one hundred years ago in the town of Stanz there were alot of poor boys who had neither mother nor father. They had lost them in war. Now it came about that these poor boys should have a school. So in the town of Stanz there was a convent and it only had one room in it. Well the people thought that this room would do becaus the people themselves were very poor.

This class room was neither larg nor comfortable but anyway the people were even glad for this. The man who had charge of the school was an old man but he was very fond of children. He had a very hard time in teaching these children for their were never in school befor. The old man promised to teach and live with the children. He was like a father to them. They had to sleep and eat and study in the same room.

He would play with the boys at playtime so as to make them happy and was also very kind to them.

It happen that children was not in this school no longer than a year when war broke out again. The war broke out right near Stanz and a battle was fought. There was quite a few soldiers wounded and the people were to poor to have a hospital. So the general seeing that the only thing to do was to go and asked to people of Stanz to let them have it. So he went and asked the old man. and he let them have it. So the only school was changed into a hospital.

Original Story.

A SCHOOL FOR POOR BOYS.

I am going to read a short story to you, and then I shall ask you to write one of your own about it.

About a hundred years ago, there existed, in the town of Stanz, in Switzerland, a little school. It had been opened for the purpose of giving a home to a number of very poor boys, who had lost their parents during a terrible war.

The place in which the school was kept was neither large nor comfortable. It consisted of a single room in an old convent; but the people of Stanz themselves were poor, and it was the best home that they could provide for these orphans.

The school was in charge of a kind old man, who was very fond of children. When it was opened, he offered to keep house for the little ones, and at the same time to be their teacher.

As children were not obliged to go to school in those days, the teacher had a great deal of trouble in getting his pupils to learn. At first they did not like him, because he made them work. But as soon as they discovered that what he did was for their own good, they began to love and obey him.

As only a single room had been given to them to live in, this one room had to be used for everything. In it they had their school, took their meals, and slept. The teacher was always with them, and acted as their companion. He not only taught them, and helped them with their tasks, but also entered into their games, and often amused them by telling them stories. Indeed, he did everything he could to make them happy and to lead them to forget how poor they were.

But it so happened that the children were not allowed to remain long under this roof. Before they had been in the house a year, war broke out again. One day a battle was fought near Stanz, and a number of wounded soldiers were brought into the town. Unfortunately, the officer who was in charge of them found that there was only one place in which they could be sheltered. It was the school-room in the convent. He then came to the teacher and sorrowfully told him what he needed. So the school-room was turned into a hospital, and the poor children were obliged to give up the little home that they had learned to love so well.

(The teacher may write on the board the words "Stanz" and "Switzerland." The children in the lower grades should be told that Switzerland is in Europe.)

A discussion of the causes of the variations in the results obtained in the different schools will now be in order. The items in the table bearing upon this topic are:

1. The amount of time devoted to language in the various schools;

2. The average age of the pupils in the individual grades; and

3. The nationality and environment of the pupils.

1. As to time, the figures in the table are not to be accepted as final. They were computed from replies to printed questions distributed to the teachers after the test was taken, and are subject to revision upon closer study. But taking them temporarily just as they are—and we shall not go very far wrong by doing so—we find, as in spelling and arithmetic, that there is no direct relation between time and results, that superior results cannot be

attributed to unusual pressure, or inferior results to lack of pressure. As the figures speak for themselves, it will not be necessary for me to dilate upon this point; and I merely wish to add here that as long as the same principle appears to apply to all branches investigated, we may now safely accept the proposition that if reasonable results do not follow upon a reasonable appropriation of time, the fault lies in the teaching and not in the time-table. In spelling, the time limit within which reasonable results may be expected was fixed by my data at fifteen minutes daily, and in arithmetic at forty-five minutes. In deciding upon a time limit in language, it will be necessary to consider both oral and written work; and as the whole question borders very closely upon that of methods and devices, I shall defer its discussion to the next chapter.

2. In studying the relation of age to results in language, we find, on looking at the general averages, that, as might naturally be expected, the results rise invariably from one grade to the next. However, it will be seen that the ascent is by no means a regular one. From the fourth grade to the fifth, the advance is from 6.8 to 12.2, or 5.4 per cent; between the fifth and the sixth, the rise is from 12.2 to 23.2, or 11.0 per cent; between the sixth and the seventh, it is from 23.2 to 30.6, or 7.4 per cent; and between the seventh and the eighth, it is from 30.6 to 47.0, or 16.4 per cent. These figures look innocent enough, but I have never seen so many suggestive points crowded into so small a compass. For example, a general average of 6

per cent in the fourth grade, 12 in the fifth, and 23 in the sixth suggests the sending of a relief expedition in search of the innumerable first and second year literary prodigies who must have been blown out of their course after steering successfully out of the second grade. Again, the comparatively insignificant gain between the sixth and seventh years suggests an inquiry into the cause of the weakness in seventh year work, a weakness that was manifested in my test in arithmetic as well. And there is also an inquiry suggested by the rapid rise from the seventh to the eighth year, which in the general average is equal to that of any two previous years, and in the case of the second and third schools is equal to that of the three preceding years.

But leaving these points for future discussion, and comparing the results of the different schools from the standpoint of age, we find that the pupils in the schools at the lower end of the table are, on the whole, somewhat younger than those in the schools at the upper end, and that the pupils in the last school are the youngest of all. Still, these differences do not clear up the situation, because the theory of age will not hold when the individual schools are compared with one another. To cite but a single instance, the average age in the eighth grade of the second school is just the same as that in the eighth grade of the tenth, while the results are 76.2 against 40.5.

But should not some allowance be made for the last school, in view of the fact that its pupils are the youngest? I answer, emphatically: By no means. The pupils of any given grade must be judged by the standards of that grade; and if they cannot compete with others on the same basis, they do not belong where they are. There would be no art in devising a system of promotion whereby the pupils, as a class, would be enabled to graduate from the grammar school even at the age of twelve. But would they then be grammar school graduates in the true sense of the word, or would they merely be primary school graduates bearing a grammar-school label?

3. In regard to nationality and environment, I desire to explain that the figures in the column representing the percentage of American parentage do not exhaust my data on the subject, but are intended to be merely suggestive. Knowing the stress that is generally laid upon these factors in considering results in language, I have made a rather close inquiry in regard to their different phases, and shall publish the details later.

Speaking not only from the figures in Table I, but also from other data, and from my personal knowledge of the schools, my conclusion is that home environment is somewhat of a factor in the matter of written English, but by no means as important a one as it is generally supposed to be. In its favor, I am able to say that in six of the seven schools that have been classed as satisfactory, the children are largely from American homes; [1] and, of these

[[1] The figures for the seventh school are not given in the table, but, judging by the neighborhood, I should say that the American parentage was upward of 80 per cent. Under American parentage I have classed those pupils only whose

six schools, five are distinctly "aristocratic." But this point is offset by two others, which are sufficient to prove that the power to use good English in writing may be developed without special home culture, and that home culture will not in itself suffice to lead to the desired end.

As to the first of these points, it may be said that while five of the seven satisfactory schools are of the "aristocratic" type, two are not. In the second school, 71 per cent of the pupils are of American parentage, it is true; but the building is situated in a rather poor district, and the home culture is certainly not above the average. And the fourth school, it will be seen, is very largely foreign, not more than 28 per cent of the pupils coming from American homes.

In regard to the second point, it is to be noted that the home conditions are at least up to the average in the schools that rank tenth, twelfth, fourteenth, sixteenth, seventeenth, nineteenth, and twentieth. And it is of particular interest to note that the school in which the American parentage is as low as 6 per cent stands ninth, thus outranking seven schools attended by pupils whose home advantages are not inferior to those of the second school in the table.

However, taking all the pros and cons into consideration, it seems to me that a school attended

parents were American or English and who heard no foreign language at home. If a foreign language was spoken at home, I classed the pupils as foreign, even when both parents were American.]

largely by children of foreigners is laboring somewhat at a disadvantage, and that some allowance should be made for the handicap; but I think that a fair allowance would be 1 per cent in the school average for every 10 per cent of foreign parentage.

XI

ENGLISH (CONTINUED). THE NEED OF A NEW BASIS IN EDUCATION [1]

In the preparation of the present chapter, which is intended primarily to offer a fundamental explanation of the fact that some seventy per cent of the schools examined in arithmetic and language failed to show even a moderate degree of success in those branches—which, in the eyes of the general public, constitute the corner-stone of a practical education—I did not lose sight of the fact that my deductions, to be of value, would have to be based upon the assurance that the papers in both subjects had been accurately marked. As to arithmetic, no serious question can be raised from this point of view; but in language my system of computing class averages was novel, and I did not feel inclined to accept it myself without the closest of critical scrutiny, although from the standpoint of opinions, it had been approved by a number of practical educators to whom it had been demonstrated before the article was published. In brief, as I have acquired the habit of judging matters from the standpoint of facts, I did not feel justified in looking upon the method as sound unless it should be able to withstand a test in the light of facts as well. By the

[1] January-March, 1904.

system employed, the individual errors had been disregarded, and each paper judged as a unit, solely by impression; and the question arose in my mind whether the impression made by a paper was, after all, a reliable indication of its merit, or whether accurate criticism did not demand a careful analysis of each paper in the light of actual errors.

The problem suggested by this question could not be contemplated with equanimity. I had already read the fourth and fifth grade papers once, and the sixth, seventh, and eighth grade papers twice, so that I felt no ardent desire to look them over again. Besides, the marking of a paper with precision requires very careful study of every phrase and sentence, both individually and in relation to the whole; and this means, of course, extremely slow progress. Indeed, it was soon found that even a paper that read well could not be marked minutely in less than fifteen or twenty minutes, while one that read very poorly could scarcely be marked in less than an hour. Under these circumstances, I was, of course, obliged to abandon the idea of putting all the papers through the mill. So I did the next best thing and selected for examination certain typical sets, amounting in all to some 2,000 papers.

However, in order to enhance the value of the work, I appreciated the advisability of not only counting the number of errors, but of classifying them as well, with a view to pointing out to teachers the most frequent sources of error. Therefore, as a preliminary to the marking, I decided to complete a system of classification. With this in mind,

I took in hand paper after paper and noted each error as I encountered it. Finally, after considerable effort, I felt that I had developed a practical working basis. The number of classes of errors had by that time mounted to ninety-three; and while this number did not by any means cover them all, I believed that it would answer the purpose.

The preliminaries having been completed, the examination of the papers was begun. But I had not proceeded beyond the marking of twenty compositions before it became perfectly evident that there was no direct relation between the number of errors contained in a paper and its literary merit, and that, for comparative purposes, the tabulation of the number of errors per hundred words would be not only absolutely worthless, but altogether misleading.

The flaw did not lie in the classification, which was perfectly practical as far as it had gone. The difficulty was simply due to the fact that the errors in the compositions differed very markedly in degree; that some of them were so strikingly bad as apparently to cover the entire field of vision; that others were scarcely noticeable except on careful reading or actual analysis; while, finally, any number of expressions were encountered that really called for the weight of authority to decide whether they should be looked upon as right or wrong. In brief, it was found almost at the outset that we cannot mark a composition as we mark a paper in spelling or arithmetic. In spelling, one error is, for all practical purposes, as bad as another, so that, in giving a test of fifty words, we simply take off two for each misspelled word, and the marking becomes automatic. In arithmetic, also, we can agree upon a system of grading and follow it automatically. But in language it is no exaggeration to say that some errors are ten or even twenty times as bad as others; and a system of marking upon a basis of actual errors would have to take this fact into consideration. The truth is that papers containing the same number of errors could vary in degree from marked literary merit to veritable rubbish.

In view of what has been stated, it would be natural to suppose that we could be helped out of the dilemma by grading the errors in accordance with their class. But the fact is that even if such a tedious process could be consistently carried out, only little would be gained thereby, because errors of the same class may also vary markedly in degree. While errors of certain varieties are always great, those of others are sometimes slight and sometimes great, so that mere numbers would here tell us nothing, because we should not know how many times the errors of the latter varieties had been slight and how frequently they had been great. Concrete examples could be furnished *ad libitum;* but as it would take us too far to enter into details here, I shall omit the discussion of this question.

But comparisons by numbers of errors could not really convey the truth even if my ninety-three classes should be so minutely subdivided as to permit of the tabulation of the exact degree of each flaw. This is due to the fact that in language it is necessary to consider the positive as well as the negative side, for the positive side also varies greatly in degree. In spelling, words that are not wrong are perfect; and in arithmetic, answers that are not wrong are perfect. But this is not true of language; for, theoretically, an entire composition may be free of flaws and yet be very poor, while, on the other hand, it may contain a number of errors and still be exceptionally good. Therefore, in criticising a literary production on a mathematical scale, it would be necessary to note the credits as well as the debits, to strike a balance, and, finally, to mark the papers so many points plus or minus, representing the surplus or the deficit. On the debit side, there would have to be posted the actual number of errors and the degree of each; and on the credit side, we should have to post the degree of merit in command of language, sentence construction, flow of language, euphony, artistic taste, interpretation of thought, logic, clearness of ideas, originality, sentiment, and a host of other things.

In brief, after a long and circuitous course in search of a scientific system of marking, I have become convinced that a composition must be judged as a unit, just as we judge a picture or any other work of art, by impression, and therefore that my system of marking was not only permissible for the purpose for which it was intended, but that, in principle, it stands for the only fair basis of comparison. Consequently, I feel justified in accepting as a practical working basis the percentages published in the preceding chapter, and in founding upon them the deductions concerning the causes of success and of failure.

One other question has been suggested, namely, whether my test was such as to bring out the real conditions, or whether a different test might not have produced different results. As to this, I desire to say that while a test of a different nature would no doubt result in a different scale of percentages, I cannot conceive of a test that would serve to reverse the comparative standing of the schools. It has been said that possibly the schools that received the high percentages had been doing a great deal of reproduction work, while those that failed had been laboring on other lines. In answer I need merely say that only a moderate amount of reproduction work had been done in the former schools, that, in fact, but little of it had been done in any of the schools above the sixth year. And as to the fact that the test called for the first draft, it is interesting to note that the pupils of the class that did the finest work had not been accustomed to present the first draft to their teacher, so that the test was no less unusual to them than it was to any of the other pupils examined.

As the first draft only was accepted, there is no doubt that the test was severe, and that the classes that did poorly would have done better if they had had an opportunity to revise their copy. However, I do not see how this could have affected the relative position of the schools. That children who do poorly on a severe test are likely to do better on an easier one is a reasonable assumption; but I cannot entertain the proposition that pupils who do remarkably well on a difficult test are likely to fail on an easy one. Moreover, through subsequent visits to many of the schools, during which I had an opportunity to interview teachers, I became convinced in more ways than one that the best work was done by the pupils who had been in the habit of doing the best daily work, and that their superior power would show on any piece of writing that they should be at any time asked to do.

We are now ready to enter upon the discussion of the main theme of this chapter, namely, the reasons why the schools, on the whole, failed to make a better showing, and what can be done to improve their prospects.

To call the question of the causes of success or of failure in elementary education one of the most important of all pedagogical problems would be very far short of the truth; for it is, in fact, the problem of problems, embracing them all in one. It involves the question of the characteristics of pupils, of the individuality, education, and training of teachers, of the entire province of supervision, and of school organization and administration. And, to gain a clear insight into the problem of causes, each of these factors must be studied in turn, and its relative influence determined.

In searching through the category of possible causes of success in some instances and of failure in others, I have found it necessary to exclude one plausible theory after another by reason of its failure to explain the facts; but I have finally come upon a theory that not only seems to hold its own when examined in the light of facts, but which appears to account for the circumstance that all other theories, however plausible, were found to vanish when exposed to the light. The theory is simply this, that success in teaching, as measured by results, is primarily dependent upon something inherent in the teaching, the nature of which will become clear as we proceed.

I have come to this conclusion, because it offers a hypothesis which is perfectly capable of explaining any number of phenomena which, though apparently incredible, have been strikingly in evidence in every subject thus far investigated, playing havoc with all our preconceived notions, and casting them to the winds. For example, the tables have furnished an abundance of evidence to prove that there is no direct relation between the time devoted to a subject and the results; the facts having shown conclusively that certain specified results could be obtained within a certain specified limit of time, provided a certain unknown element was brought into play, but that, in the absence of that element, the desired results would not be accomplished even if the time should be inordinately increased beyond the specified limit. The fact itself was not at first startling, because, *a priori*, it could be accounted for in so many ways; but the surprises began to accumulate when one common-sense reason after another was examined and found wanting.

It has always been supposed that the size of the class must necessarily exert a powerful influence on the results. But investigation showed that there was no relation between the size of the class and the results, that some of the best work had been done in the largest classes, and some of the poorest in the smallest classes. It has also been accepted as an axiom that the results are largely influenced by the heredity, nationality, and home environment of the pupils. But in spelling and arithmetic, these factors appeared to play a very insignificant part, if any; while even in language, where they have always been supposed to control the helm, they were found to exert an exceedingly small amount of influence as compared with that of the magic elixir. Nor could the differences in results be accounted for by differences in scholarship or in knowledge of pedagogical theory, on the part of the teachers, because teachers of practically equal qualifications, from a theoretical standpoint, produced widely different results. And after the publication of the preceding article, I looked closely into the methods employed in teaching English, in the schools that I had examined, only to find, however, that among teachers using practically identical methods some had met with marked success, while others had utterly failed. In a word, it appears that where the desired element is present in sufficient quantity, success will be attained in spite of unfavorable conditions and apparently unscientific methods, and that where it falls below a certain minimum, the results will be poor, even if the conditions should favor the teacher, the methods should be of the most scientific order, the appointments should be made by merit instead of by pull, and the members of the school board should be elected by districts instead of by wards.

The conclusion that the attainment of satisfactory results is primarily a question of a certain specific thing in the teaching appears so extremely elementary that my researches might seem to have been unnecessary. However, when looked upon in the light of my data, it not only overthrows our preconceived notions in regard to points already enumerated, but it serves to upset certain favorite educational doctrines as well. The suggestion that the nature of the teaching is the ultimate cause of success seems to favor the traditional belief that the teacher is born and not made, which, however, is controverted by the facts, as I shall presently show. But, as we shall see, it also seems to conflict with the modern belief that the teacher is made and not born, although there is in this respect a delusion.

The theory that the teacher is born and not made is disproved by the fact that the results do not bear a direct relation to the native ability of the teachers. If native ability were the determining element, we should have to find marked irregularity in the results obtained in the different class-rooms of the same school building, and but little variation in the results of different buildings taken as a whole. But, in fact, the reverse of this is the case; for the striking differences are not found in the different class-rooms of the same building. They do not begin to appear until the results of one building are compared with those of another. This seems to prove that the teaching faculty is not limited to a favored few, but that it is subject to development in normal individuals generally, though, of course, in varying degree; and that it is developed in some schools, while permitted to lie dormant in others.

What has just been said is, of course, a point in favor of those who believe in training. But on looking at the facts from their side of the case, we find ourselves again perplexed; for, as has been already stated, it has been impossible to trace any direct relation between professional qualifications, as generally understood, and results. It is this that points to the delusion, which lies in the fact that professional qualifications as generally understood, namely, a knowledge of psychology and pedagogy, combined with scholarship, do not in themselves constitute the elements that assure the attainment of satisfactory results. Indeed, the fact that a knowledge of psychology and pedagogy does not make the teacher, even when combined with scholarship, is so universally appreciated among practical school people that no argument is required to substantiate it.

Now, if the problem of successful teaching has resolved itself into the problem of developing the ability to attain results, and if experience has shown that the study of psychology and pedagogy, even when combined with culture, has not sufficed to bring about the desired development, then we cannot avoid the conclusion that the methods of development thus far employed have not sufficed to accomplish the purpose, and that something more must be done before training can be made to hit the mark.

And now we are ready for the crucial questions: (1) How can we account for the fact that the study of the educational sciences has failed to serve the purpose? and (2) What is the specific form of training required to bring about the desired end? Let us consider these questions in turn.

That the new ideals are not only higher than the old, but absolutely fundamental, and must in time prevail, is not even open to question; and, strange as it may seem, they are the very same ideals upheld by the identical public that has always so strongly protested against surrendering the schools to the educational reformers, namely, greater intelligence and greater efficiency. Consequently, the people are not at loggerheads with the new education in the matter of ideals, but they are opposed to it because they not only fail to perceive the manifestation of that greater intelligence and greater efficiency which the new school has promised to produce, but are inclined to believe that the graduates of our elementary schools are even less intelligent and less efficient than they were under the old régime.

Why, then, has training failed to give a better account of itself? My answer is that training has failed to produce better results because it has not been followed by a specific demand for better results. On the contrary, it has been accompanied by a mandate to despise results. This has arisen from the belief that the results produced by the more rational methods of instruction are purely spiritual in their nature and incapable of measurement, and, conversely, that results which can be demonstrated in any definite manner must have been produced by methods that should be avoided. In other words, ordinary training has failed because it has been founded upon the assumption—not verified by experience—namely, that certain forms of pedagogical treatment are sure to lead to ideal results. The consequence has been that the educators of the new school have become accustomed to gauge the success of a teacher from the standpoint of what she does, while in matters outside of school success is measured by what is accomplished. By reason of this unpractical stand, the demand has been developing in the direction of methods and mannerisms which may or may not contribute to success, but which in themselves do not constitute success, and are not even a gauge of it; and in the effort to meet this demand, the fundamental issue, actual accomplishment, has become entirely submerged.

Therefore, in accordance with the trend of the times, it has become the custom to call a teacher successful if her methods are in the latest style, if her manners are pleasant, and if her pupils show an interest in the current lesson; while a teacher is placed on a lower plane if she does not come up to all these requirements. But this position is untenable. One who makes the impression that she is all that a successful teacher ought to be may be a successful teacher in fact, or she may be lacking in certain essential elements involved in good teaching, and fail to accomplish much in the end. On the other hand, a teacher who does not make a favorable impression may in fact be a poor teacher, but not necessarily so, for she may be possessed of just those qualities which are essential to success, and may therefore accomplish far more than her more brilliant colleague.

In view of the above considerations, the answer to the second question is obvious. The current method of training having failed by reason of a false standard of measuring success, the remedy lies in substituting for it a more scientific one. The current standard calls for an estimate of success by what the teacher does, and the one now suggested will call for judgment by what she accomplishes. Of course, such a radical change in the standard would not only carry with it a change in demand, but also the necessity of revising our conception of pedagogical training, which would have to be more definitely directed toward the development of the power to achieve results. But just as the demand for an ideal class-room spirit has served to bring about a markedly better spirit, so the demand for ideal results would undoubtedly be followed by better work and start the schools on the road to a still higher ideal, namely, the combination of an ideal spirit with ideal results.

The theory that success in teaching should be judged by results is, of course, anything but a novel one; and in view of the pedagogical abuses to which it has led, and the just condemnation it has received at the hands of many, it may seem strange that any one should have the hardihood not merely to indorse it, but to suggest it as a fundamental truth. However, the fact is that we are here again brought face to face with a pedagogical proposition which is correct in principle, but which has ended in disaster by reason of a misconception. In a word, the traditional system of measuring success by results has proved a signal failure, because those who have followed it have failed to appreciate that results differ widely in quality, that some are of a high and others of a low order, in consequence of which they have become accustomed to accept as satisfactory a class of results which neither indicate genuine teaching nor satisfy the demands of an intelligent public. The standard that I am suggesting represents a demand for results on a much higher plane, but recognizes at the same time that such results must be based on a firmer foundation than faith.

As to the specific difference between a low and a high order of results, this cannot be accurately explained in any general statement, for every branch must be considered on its own merits. However, taking a broad view of the matter, it may be said that in the former the dominant idea is knowledge, knowledge of facts and of certain formal processes, while in the latter it is efficiency, the ability to think and to utilize knowledge in thought and execution. As knowledge is a matter of memory, and can be acquired without bringing into play, to any considerable extent, the exercise of the higher mental faculties, it so happens that up to a certain point a great deal may be accomplished simply by getting pupils to study their lessons and to be attentive during the recitations. Consequently, it is evident that, within a given compass, children who have but slightly exercised their higher mental faculties may be able to compete on an equal footing with those who for years have had the more genuine forms of mental training. However, if we recognize that, within certain limits, children who have had no genuine teaching are able to compete with those who have been very well taught, we must also recognize that when these limits have been reached the contrast between good and poor teaching will begin to tell in the results.

This suggests in a nutshell both the flaw and the remedy. The trouble with the traditional standards has been that they have aimed to measure success within the limits of the lower area; and the remedy lies in instituting standards that will take as their starting-point the upper limit of the lower area. That is to say, the higher order of standards, ideally speaking, will give no credits for mechanical results, but simply for such results as show a true indication of intelligence and efficiency. Tests formulated upon the higher basis will, however, by no means overlook essential facts and processes of a mechanical order, because pupils must necessarily be thoroughly grounded in the fundamentals to be able to pass the higher tests. As children have brains, they cannot, of course, help acquiring some efficiency as a result of the acquisition of knowledge, however poorly they may be taught; so that in testing for efficiency a part of the credit for that which is manifested will belong to the pupils. Nevertheless, my investigations have brought to light the fact that children do not acquire much of it unaided, but that it is primarily a matter of training; for otherwise the tremendous differences in the results obtained in different schools could not have occurred.

As every subject presents its own peculiarities and must be considered on its own merits, it would be a mere assumption on my part to state in how many of the common school branches the line of discrimination between the higher and the lower order of results could be safely drawn. However, I am able to say, and I shall illustrate the fact, that the line may be rather clearly drawn in the two subjects which not only consume much of the time spent in school, but which count for so much in practical affairs that the reformer may reform to his heart's content if he will but do his duty here. They are: (1) arithmetic, which is a world in itself; and (2) language, which includes so many things in one. At the outset, I did not anticipate that much could be done with the inductive work beyond the domain of the three R's; and to what extent other branches could be brought within its range and within that of its logical outcome is still an open question.

The proposition that intellectual strength is subject to measurement suggests the inductive study not only of educational results, but of that fundamental educational problem which is so largely instrumental in shaping the curriculum itself, and not only the curriculum of the elementary school, but that of the higher institutions as well, namely, the problem of the relative values of different subjects from the standpoint of mental discipline. If intellectual strength is the resultant of a combination of artificial stimuli of different varieties, and such strength is subject to measurement, then it becomes, so to say, a simple problem in dynamics to determine the degree of influence exerted by the individual stimuli, and consequently their relative values. Having made no special investigation touching upon this point, I have no reliable facts to offer. However, it is interesting to note that the data incidentally obtained during my tests in arithmetic and English appear to indicate that of the two subjects that tradition has handed down as mental trainers *par excellence*, arithmetic and grammar, arithmetic merits the position it has won, while grammar does not. This statement is based upon the fact that all the schools in which the pupils had displayed a high degree of intelligence in arithmetic also produced very creditable work in that great intellectual barometer, English composition, while composition was frequently at a very low ebb where the pupils were apparently well versed in grammar. This information is not offered in the nature of a conclusion, but simply as suggesting an entering wedge into the study of a different problem.

Having found that, from a practical standpoint, genuine educational progress means neither more nor less than the development of a higher order of measurable results, the practical pedagogical problem becomes resolved into that of devising ways and means destined to lead to this much-desired end; and it is to the matter of ways and means that I shall now direct attention. However, owing to the magnitude of the subject, I shall not attempt to enter into its innumerable ramifications, but shall confine my remarks to a few statements concerning the two fundamental conditions of success: (1) A well-defined, but reasonable, minimum demand, based, first, upon a clear conception of the ideal end, and, secondly, upon a knowledge of what a fairly good teacher is able to accomplish in the desired direction; and (2) a clearly defined method of judging to what extent each teacher is meeting that demand. Expressing these ideas in homely phraseology, we have the simple proposition that the essential conditions of success in pedagogy, as elsewhere, are *to know what you want and to see that you get it.*

Up to the present time, the new school of education has not had more than a general conception of what results it really desires to attain, and consequently has not had even a foundation upon which to base a specific demand in the light of the new ideals. Therefore, the accusation that the modern school is trying to destroy the good in the old without putting anything definite in its place is not altogether unwarranted. That the traditional demands have led to all sorts of pedagogical abuses cannot be doubted; but this does not justify the assumption that pedagogical demands are wrong in principle. The law of demand and supply is fundamental and cannot be argued out of existence; and what is needed to insure progress is not the destruction of a much-abused fundamental principle, but a detailed specification of what results may be expected, from grade to grade, in the march toward the ideal goals, and the development of demands in accordance with what experience has proved to be feasible.

Let us now see in what particulars the new ideals differ from the old, and how the demands may be changed to keep pace with them.

In touching upon this point, I stated that, generally speaking, the lower results were represented by knowledge and the higher results by efficiency. But, with a view to the practical, the same idea may be more readily appreciated if we accept as a basis that the higher results in any given branch are represented by the realization of the purpose for which it is taught, while the lower results are represented by the knowledge and skill acquired on the road to the higher end. Therefore, the higher demand in each individual subject must be based, fundamentally, upon a clear conception of its purpose, and the minimum demand upon the extent to which that purpose can be realized, from grade to grade, by fairly efficient teachers, laboring under ordinary conditions. As the difference between mechanical and ideal results was very clearly demonstrated by my tests in arithmetic and language, it may be of interest to take these subjects as illustrations.

In arithmetic the purpose is clear. It is, so to say, to get the children to understand the relation of numbers and how to combine them. In order to arrive at this end, it is necessary to acquire a knowledge of a large number of processes and principles, and to learn how to apply that knowledge through practice in concrete problems. Now a test at the end of a given period may have one of two things in view. Its object may be to discover how well the pupils are conversant with the processes and principles they have studied, and whether they have acquired facility in the solution of problems in line with those in which they have been drilled; or its object may be to learn to what extent the pupils have acquired the ability to apply their knowledge of processes and principles in the solution of varieties of problems in which they have not been drilled. The former represents a memory test, in which poorly taught children are able to compete with those who have had the benefit of genuine teaching, while the latter is a test of the power to reason, and should result in a victory for the superior teaching.

Now my own test in arithmetic was so formulated as to give no credit whatever for a knowledge of processes and principles, nor did it take into account what kind of problems had received particular attention in individual schools. It simply consisted of a series of problems coming within the scope of all the pupils, but making a knowledge of the fundamentals indispensable to success. This test not only brought to light an enormous difference in arithmetical ability in different schools, but also the fact that this difference increased with the ascent of the grades, until in the eighth year the results varied almost from zero to perfection, the extremes in the class averages being 11.3 and 93.9 per cent, respectively. This indicates that the effect of training the reasoning faculties is cumulative, that under its influence much ability may be developed during the elementary school period, and that in the schools where reliance is placed mainly on the memory, the reasoning faculties fail to react when confronted by a test of any degree of severity. In truth, in a few of the schools, the problems whose formulæ had not been studied might almost as well have been presented in Greek.

But what is perhaps more surprising still is the fact that, in the schools that utterly collapsed on my test, there had never been even a suspicion of weakness, for the teachers here as elsewhere had been accustomed to obtain class averages of eighty to ninety per cent on tests that they or their superintendents had formulated. In the light of what I have stated, the discrepancy is easily explained: Their home-made tests were memory tests, and the pupils had become accustomed to work arithmetic by formula; while in the schools where true ability was demonstrated, the home-made tests were tests of ability, and the children had become accustomed to work arithmetic by the aid of their reasoning faculties. The new ideals call for the development of the power to think, and the new demands must follow on the same line. And it seems to me that in formulating tests in accordance with the new ideals, we should be guided as far as possible by the principle of calling upon the pupils to do things that they have never done before, in contradistinction to the old rule not to ask them to do what they have not been directly taught to do.

When we turn our attention from arithmetic to language, we encounter a far different kind of problem; for arithmetic has but a single purpose, while language has a multiplicity of purposes, the most prominent among which are: (1) The study of the structure of language (technical grammar); (2) the development of the ability to interpret thought; and (3) the development of the ability to express ideas in correct and readable English.

That language has more purposes than one has been thoroughly understood from time immemorial; but what has not been recognized in practice is the fact that its different phases, though members of the same family and mutually helpful, are separate entities; that they must be developed on independent lines; that one of them cannot be accepted as a substitute for another; that we have no right to assume that one of them can be developed through exercise in another; and that the degree of development of one cannot be estimated by the degree of development of another.

It would be foreign to my purpose to enter into a discussion concerning the relative value of the different phases of language work from an academic point of view. However, speaking from the popular standpoint, it is perfectly safe to say not only that written English takes the first rank in language, but that the development of the ability to write ranks first among all subjects taught in the elementary school. As the power to express one's thoughts in correct and readable language has not been exalted by our own people alone, but by those of other countries as well, the idea cannot be looked upon as a mere fad, but must rest upon a real basis of some kind or another. And that basis, it seems to me, is not that the people desire to fit their children for a literary career, but the fact that written language constitutes the only popular means of judging what the elementary school is doing for the child. Nor is this view to be stamped as narrow; for even in the highest educational circles the feeling has been developing that written language is not merely what it stands for in the elementary school curriculum—one-third of one of a dozen branches—but that it is largely representative of the character of the training that the child has received as a whole; that it is a general manifestation not only of knowledge of English, but of knowledge in general, and not only of knowledge, but of thought power, logic, understanding, taste, sentiment, precision, and so on; that it is, in fact, as I have already expressed it, the barometer of elementary education; and to the extent to which that barometer rises will rise the confidence in our educators.

But the popular demand for improvement in expression does not run counter to the new ideals. On the contrary, the development of the art of expression is a cardinal principle in the new education; and this has been manifested in practice by the fact that the most attention has been given to expression—not only in the manual arts, but in English as well—in the schools in charge of the most radical educators. In consequence of this attitude toward English on the part of progressive educators, and in view of the fact that the general educational trend is progressive, composition, in its various phases, has been for many years prosecuted with vigor in some communities, and has received a fair amount of attention in most of the others; and still the people continue to complain, not without justice, that the English in our schools is lamentably weak.

But why has this increase in effort failed to lead to a more decided improvement? This again may be explained by the fact that the higher ideal has not been accompanied by a specific demand for better results. In truth, the initial steps have not yet been taken to arrive at a basis upon which a higher demand could be formulated. Before we can make a genuine effort to get what we want, we must, in the first instance, know what we want, and we must also know how much we can get. But in written language no one is able to express in terms what we have had, or what we have now, or what we can get, as no attempt has ever been made—except, perhaps, the test upon which this chapter is based—to make out a statement of the actual conditions.

And how may this lack of definiteness be accounted for? The explanation here also is near at hand. The radical educators have not even attempted to develop any standards, because they do not believe that efficiency can be demonstrated by means of tests. True to their creed, they have simply adhered to the motto that we learn to do by doing, and have forged ahead confident in the belief that their methods would make it all right in the end.

But if the radicals have done nothing in this direction, those who have retained their faith in measurable results have done even worse than nothing, for they have actually stood in the way of the development of genuine standards by laboring under artificial and spurious ones, which are not only too low, but positively deluding. They have gradually come to recognize, it is true, that the art of expression must be fostered in school; but they have made the great mistake of overlooking the fact that the development of the power of expression does not simply represent a new chapter in an old and familiar book, but a new and independent subject, which must follow a course of its own.

As a result of this error, the introduction of the art of expression into the curriculum has not been followed by an independent demand for the development of the power of expression, but has simply been treated in the light of another addition to technical grammar. The truth of this assertion is illustrated by the fact that the typical examination paper in English to-day represents a mixture of everything that is known *inside* of the school as "language," of which the art of expression is one. And what is wrong with this? Nothing beyond the fact that under an arrangement of this kind it is possible to roll up class averages of eighty to ninety per cent in language where the art of expression—or language as the term is commonly understood *outside* of school—is in a most deplorable state. This was abundantly demonstrated by my own test, which, as a pure and simple test of the power of expression, caused the utter collapse of all structures that had been artificially propped up by technical grammar and all kinds of devices under the sun.

I do not wish to be understood by this as casting a vote against the study of technical grammar in the elementary school. Indeed, I do not see how the teacher can guide her pupils in their composition work without a reference to grammar. But I do wish to impress the fact that grammar—*i.e.*, from the standpoint of composition—is merely one of any number of forces that aid in the development of the power of expression, and cannot be looked upon as a substitute for, or a gauge of, the ability to write. And what is true of grammar, from this particular point of view, is equally true of everything else included under language in the elementary school course. In a word, the only test of the power of expression is a test of the power of expression, and, in the interest of progress in practical English, composition should be examined as a thing apart.

But this does not mean that composition is from this time on to run riot in our schools. In fact, if I had the say in the matter, I should not set aside any more time for language *in toto* than is now devoted to it. Nor is any fault to be found with the ways and means at present employed by our most successful teachers, which are deserving of detailed discussion. The sum and substance of the matter is this, that satisfactory results in the art of expression can be obtained by devoting not more than forty-five to fifty minutes a day to language, including everything now taught under that caption, and that failure to produce a certain minimum of ability within that limit of time must be attributed to a weakness in the teaching—not necessarily in the teaching of English alone, but possibly in the whole round of teaching.

Space will not permit me to continue this line of discussion into other elementary-school branches; but I shall show in closing that, as in arithmetic and language, so in the training of teachers, the shortcomings have been due to a failure to discriminate between knowledge and efficiency, and a confusion of means and ends. In a word, the mistake has here been made of accepting a knowledge of psychology and pedagogy, which must be classed among the means to the end, as the equivalent of the ability to teach, which is the real end of training. Psychology and pedagogy do not in themselves constitute more than mere memory studies, so that they come within the domain of that lower area in which the weakest may meet the strongest on the same footing, a circumstance which renders possible a condition similar to that which was found in arithmetic and language, namely, ninety per cent in knowledge of pedagogy and ten per cent in the ability to teach.

If we recognize that the supreme end of pedagogy is the development of the power to teach, or the power to develop power in the pupil, and that this power must be regarded as the one specific energy capable of driving the educational wheels, then we must look upon the *knowledge* possessed by the teacher, whether of psychology, pedagogy, history, literature, or what not, merely as her store of raw material, in which the energy is pent up in a latent state. Under these circumstances, the problem of training becomes simply the problem of developing the greatest amount of energy out of a given amount of raw material. And the keynote to development is exactly the same in the mental as it has been in the physical world. In the latter, progress has been brought about by overcoming the difficulties of one task and following that task with a more difficult one, and so on, until the apparently impossible of half a century ago has come to be mere child's play today. In education, to begin with, it would simply be necessary to see that the school in our block shall develop as much power in its pupils as is developed in the school around the corner, and next to see that the school around the corner shall develop as much power as the school across the river, etc., etc.

However, continuous progress in education cannot be secured through manufactured laws of teaching, any more than progress in engineering can be brought about through manufactured laws of physics, but depends, first, upon the recognition of a law of nature, which must be accepted as a common basis of calculation, namely, the capacity of the human mind to develop power, and, secondly, upon an advance in the minimum demand to keep pace with our ability to eliminate waste, *i.e.*, with our ability to generate more and more power with a given amount of raw material. But what *can* be secured through man-made laws, in any locality to-day, at a moment's notice, and by a trifling additional expense, is a system of supervision based upon the recognition of the fundamental law. What such a system implies will be discussed in the next chapter.

XII

THE NEED OF A NEW BASIS IN SUPERVISION [1]

In the preceding chapter, I pointed out that the marked variations in the results obtained in different schools upon my tests in arithmetic and language could not be explained by the causes to which they might naturally be supposed to be due, such as differences in the general and professional education of the teachers, in the conditions under which they were obliged to labor, in the methods employed, and so on, but that, in the ultimate analysis, they could only be accounted for on the supposition of a difference in the degree of something inherent in the nature of the teaching, as this alone appeared competent to explain the fact that in the schools in which the conditions were favorable, both in regard to the home environment of the pupils and the professional education of the teachers, the results were sometimes extremely low, while in the schools in which the conditions were very unfavorable, the results were sometimes comparatively high. Again, owing to the fact that the striking differences in the degree of success did not appear in the different class-rooms of the same building, but only when the work of a building as a whole was compared with

[1] April-June, 1904.

that of another, I contended that the power to teach was not born with the individual, but was largely a matter of development, and could be developed, to a greater or lesser extent, in the majority of normally constituted people, not, however, by our present normal-school training, which was merely a preparatory affair, but by means of certain special agencies. And if this conclusion is correct, it is evident that no system of school administration, however ideal it may appear on paper, and however worthy the officials may be, will succeed in effecting substantial and permanent improvement unless the designated factor is duly recognized and made the basis of action.

In my opinion, the most striking feature in reference to my tests is a fact which cannot be argued out of existence, namely, that the marked variations in the results were not found in the different classrooms of the same building, but in the different buildings taken as a whole. While in regard to the causes of this phenomenon it is not safe to make dogmatic statements, the conclusion is nevertheless near at hand that the most important element in the attainment of results lies in something that is inherent in the make-up of the principal, whether this be actual superiority in the training of his teachers, or sufficient modesty to give free rein to those who are stronger than himself, and permitting these to exert their good influence on the other members of the corps. However this may be, there is no doubt that, within considerable limits, the standards of efficiency are set by something inherent in the individual schools, regardless of what system of supervision may prevail.

Since the publication of the preceding article, I have been asked by a number of readers to give a more detailed explanation of the nature of what I understand by teaching power. In reply, I regret to be obliged to report that I have not yet been able to solve the mystery of mental faculties, so that I must avail myself of the usual privilege of defining a power in terms of effect. It is evident, for example, that the genuine painter possesses a power which the bungler at art does not possess. However, the existence of a specific difference between them cannot be discovered by studying the differences in their personality and education, or in their methods and habits of work, but is brought to light in one way only, namely, by the difference in the quality of their productions, the paintings of the one being works of art, while those of the other are daubs. Again, it is very well known that one person can sell more goods in an hour than another can sell in a week; but the great difference in their degree of selling power cannot be judged by a difference in their knowledge of the goods they sell, or in the amount of energy they put into their work, but is made manifest only by the difference in the value of their orders.

Now, if we know of the existence of such forces as color power, perspective power, tone power, buying power, selling power, managing power, and so on, the nature of which cannot be defined, but whose presence, in an infinite variety of forms and degrees, can only be detected through actual achievement, why have we not the right to assume that there is also such a thing as teaching power, in itself eluding analysis, but whose presence, in greater or lesser degree, and in one form or another, can only be detected in the effect produced?

If, then, we abandon the attempt to define teaching power as such, and speak of it only in terms of effect, we must call it the power to achieve success in the school-room, the power to produce a specific effect in the pupil. Now, simple as this proposition may appear, it stands in truth for nothing less than a complete transformation in our attitude toward the problem of the elementary school, shifting, as it does, our attention from the teacher to the pupil, and making the latter instead of the former, *from the standpoint of practical pedagogy*, the central figure in our educational system.

Thus, it means that while heretofore the efficiency of a teacher has been estimated primarily by her general and professional knowledge, the size of her conscience, her educational ideals, her methods, the amount of time devoted to her work outside of school hours, and so on, it must hereafter be read in the powers of the pupil, just as the power of a painter must be read in the canvas. And, in the same way, the amount of power possessed by a principal for his particular calling must be no longer estimated by the amount of experience he has had as a teacher, the number of degrees he holds, or his general interest in education, but by the proportion of his teachers who manifest a genuine ability to teach.

Again, in the case of teachers of special subjects, the fitness for a particular line of work must be no longer determined by the number of special courses they have taken, but by the degree of success attained in teaching those particular subjects. I desire to say here, in passing, that I could point to certain class-room teachers of very limited education who have taught English more successfully than certain others who have fitted themselves especially as teachers of English.

If we accept the proposition that teaching power is the power to achieve success in school work, it will be necessary, before proceeding, to define the term success; and from my point of view successful teaching is represented by the development of not less than a certain minimum of intelligence and efficiency in the pupils. This, of course, commits me to the stand that the school is primarily an institution of learning, or, rather, an institution for the training of the mind and the hand, which is evidently out of harmony with the doctrines of large numbers of present-day educators, who are apparently firmly pledged to the stand that the school is intended primarily as an institution for the training of character, while learning is only of secondary importance. Therefore, in a great many quarters, the suggestion that the efficiency of a school must be gauged, in the first instance, by the intelligence and efficiency of the pupils will be looked upon as entirely too realistic, and forthwith ruled out of court. To prove that I am in earnest, I need only call attention to the fact that no topic is more widely discussed in educational circles to-day than that concerning the ways and means of estimating the efficiency of a teacher, and to the further fact that, while all sorts of methods are suggested, few who value their reputations seem to have the courage to say that the efficiency of a teacher must be judged by what her pupils can do.

In stating my standpoint upon this question, I do not wish to be understood as implying that character development lies altogether beyond the province of the elementary school. In fact, if I could be convinced that the moral influence of teachers was inversely proportionate to their strength, that strong teaching tended to repress the good and develop the bad instinct of the child, while weak teaching did the reverse, then I should be ready to be converted. But in the absence of evidence to this effect, I shall continue to believe that weakness in the tangible work of individual schools must not be pardoned on the ground that these are laboring for the improvement of mankind and not for results that are subject to demonstration, when they are really doing nothing toward the development of the morals which is not commonly done in the schools. In a word, I believe that character development as a supplement to efficiency cannot be too warmly endorsed, but that character development as a substitute for efficiency cannot be too strongly denounced.

Proceeding, then, upon the assumption that success in teaching is represented by the development of not less than a specified minimum of intelligence and efficiency in the pupils, our problem becomes resolved into three fundamental issues, which will now be discussed in turn:

1. The selection of an educational aim capable of furnishing a theoretical basis for the development of reasonable and intelligible minimum standards.

2. The application of the theory in practice; and

3. The ways and means of enforcing the minimum when it has been developed.

1. Bearing in mind that success is dependent upon power, the aim, to be of practical value, must be one that is capable of stimulating the kind of effort which is destined to lead to the development of power. For this reason it must be neither too low nor too high. If it be too low, it will fail to stimulate effort, because no special power will be required to meet the minimum demand. And if it be placed so high as to be altogether beyond the teacher's reach, then it will equally fail to stimulate effort, because there is no object in exerting one's self in trying to grasp the unattainable. The former would be represented by an aim looking no higher than what is known as formalism; and the latter by such abstract conceptions as "the harmonious development of all the faculties," "the development of an ideal citizen," and so on, which seem to have no particular value beyond furnishing a basis for the manufacture of words, with which pedagogy is so elaborately and handsomely adorned. I therefore beg leave to submit an aim which, while keeping us rooted to terra firma, has the double advantage of offering the widest possible scope to those who de-

sire to expand, and of compelling those to exert themselves who will not move without compulsion. It may be summarized in two propositions, a theoretical and a practical one: (1) That the general aim of elementary education shall be to develop the higher faculties of the child to the full extent to which they are capable of development in the elementary school; and (2) That the actual achievement of every school shall be made to bear a reasonable relation to its possible achievement.

One who gives but a cursory glance at these two propositions may see in them nothing more than the familiar strains of a hackneyed melody. The truth is, however, that they recognize as the very foundation of elementary education, as the *sine qua non* of success and of progress, two elements which thus far have been entirely overlooked: (1) The possibilities of elementary education, *i.e.*, the extent to which it is possible to develop the various powers of the child under the limitations by which our elementary schools are governed; and (2) the necessity of taking steps to see that all children receive an education whose degree of excellence shall, at least in some measure, approach to the best that can be given to them.

The suggested basis, it seems to me, is both fair and practical. It is fair to the teachers in that it does not expect them to accomplish anything unreasonable. It is fair to the children in that it guards their interests to the extent of assuring to all a due reward for their time and effort; thus protecting them from the probability, as at present, of being consigned to schools where their most earnest efforts will be rewarded by the most meagre return. And it is practical in that it indulges in no idle dream, but simply demands that all schools laboring under certain conditions shall approach in degree of excellence the standards maintained in the moderately successful schools laboring under similar conditions. It does not ask, for example, that schools in the slums, attended by the children of foreigners, with unfavorable home surroundings, shall turn out work equal to that produced in schools attended by children from cultured American homes. It simply asks that all schools attended largely by children whose homes are poor shall in some measure approach the standards maintained in the strongest of them; and that all schools attended largely by children from cultured homes shall approach in excellence the standards maintained in the best of these, and so on.

Up to the present time, no steps have ever been taken to bring about an equal distribution of favors by means of a specific demand for the maintenance of reasonable standards in all the schools; and, in consequence, these institutions have been permitted to drift so far apart that, barring exceptional children, the weakest pupils in the strongest schools may be found, grade for grade, to be practically equal in efficiency to the strongest pupils in the weakest schools. That conditions of this nature are not characteristic of any particular type of education, but are as likely to occur under the modern as they are under the antiquated system, may be made clear by a brief explanation.

Under the traditional system, the conditions of uniform success are lacking because there is no demand for a high order of teaching. This system, it is true, has always recognized the need of working for results, and for this reason has never departed from the custom of submitting the schools to uniform examinations. But the weakness has lain in the character of the questions, which have not been prepared from the standpoint of the best that can be done for the child, but from that of the limitations of the weaker pupils of the weaker teachers. Thus, here the standards, if such they may be called, are far too low, so low, indeed, that schools may be passed as satisfactory even if bordering on demoralization.

Even in communities where the standards are low, the possibility of finding strong schools is by no means excluded, because principals who are naturally strong and zealous may far transcend the local conditions. But the demand being low, the general average is likely to be low, and some schools may lapse into a really pitiable condition. Under such a system, the difference, in the same locality, between a school good enough to pass and one in charge of an exceptionally strong principal may be nearly as great as the difference between the strongest and the weakest school in the country. In fact, in the United States, there is nothing to prevent us from finding so great a difference between two schools in neighboring districts, almost within hailing distance of each other. And the system for which I contend means simply such a change in conditions that the standards will be set by the strongest instead of the weakest schools, and that, in due course of time, no school will be passed as satisfactory whose results do not in some measure approximate those obtained in the most successful schools.

Now, admitting what I have said to be true of the traditional system, are we warranted in bringing the same charge against the schools conducted on modern lines, in which the doctrine of development is accepted as the keynote of all education? My answer must be decidedly in the affirmative; for while it cannot be denied that the ideals of the new education are very much higher than those of the old and call for a much higher order of teaching, it is no less true that, owing to a strange delusion, the educators of the modern school have failed to see the necessity of leading their teachers so to increase their power as to be able to meet the higher requirements. In a word, they have taken the delusive stand that the strength of a teacher is determined entirely by what she knows and how she teaches, and that if she knows certain things, and teaches in certain ways, she must, for that reason, be looked upon as an able teacher, even if her pupils should fail to give evidence of special ability in any direction. From this has arisen the doctrine that a teacher's success cannot be estimated by results, and that, in consequence, all uniform examinations should be abolished and all teachers should be relieved of the responsibility of accomplishing anything that is directly subject to demonstration.

Thus, if the traditional system is characterized by mechanical aims and meagre requirements, the modern system may be said to be characterized by high ideals and no requirements. In practice, this means that the advantages of the higher ideals of the new education have been offset by the disadvantages of an absence of specific demands, so that while in systems with low ideals there is nothing to prevent efficient workers from doing much better than they are required to do, in systems with high ideals, on the other hand, there is nothing to prevent inefficient workers from doing much worse than they ought to do. Consequently, in testing for results, we are apt to find in either case schools ranging from a very high to a very low grade of achievement.

Whether the modern educators are right in their claim that the children learn a great deal more in the schools where the teachers are not held responsible for results than they do in the schools where they are, or whether the people are right in contending that they learn a great deal less, is not material. The point at issue is the fact that both systems are characterized by the absence of any special obligation on the part of a principal to exert himself; so that under either condition the benefit of development in any way commensurate with natural endowment is reserved for those children whose parents, by some lucky chance, happen to reside near a building in charge of a principal who has the ability and the inclination to maintain a good school, while all other children are obliged to accept less, and some of them a great deal less, than they have a right to expect.

In view of what I have stated, it seems to me that no educational work can now compare in importance with endeavors to improve our weak and demoralized schools until they shall at least achieve what one-third of our schools are already accomplishing. This, of course, does not indicate that, in my opinion, our stronger schools are now entitled to rest on their laurels. The fact is that even these are studded with weak spots whose elimination is much to be desired. However, we may rest assured that a system of administration which should leave no stone unturned in endeavoring to elevate our weakest schools to the present standard of our strongest ones would act as a stimulus upon the latter as well, so that by the time the weaker ones had reached the goal now set for them, the strongest would have already traveled far beyond, and thus have set a new pace for those who were attempting to reach them.

It must be said at this point that, in estimating the comparative strength of schools upon a basis of results, due regard must be had for the relative importance of different subjects, and that a wise discrimination would have to be made in the allotment of credits, so that faddists would be prevented from concentrating their attention upon the less important subjects to the detriment of the more important ones. Here it will no doubt be said that such an arrangement is not feasible, because educators do not agree, and perhaps never will agree, upon the question of relative values. To this I reply that the schools do not belong to the educators, but to the people, and that upon the question of relative values the people do not disagree at all, but are now, as they have always been, practically unanimous in the assertion that the most important subjects in the curriculum are language, spelling, penmanship, and arithmetic.

Now as long as the people own the schools, and the educators are simply salaried officers, there is reason why the will of the people should prevail even if their standpoint should be altogether wrong. But that no one can say dogmatically that it is altogether wrong is proved alone by the fact that a great many reputable educators are entirely in accord with it. And I go so far as to say that the opinion of the people on the question at issue is not only defensible, but a great deal wiser than they themselves appreciate. They rest their case chiefly on the ground of utility. But I maintain, in addition, that the three R's should be made the basis in estimating the efficiency of a school, because the results in these branches are capable of presenting the most tangible evidence of the general character of instruction that the children are receiving. As practically all our schools devote enough time to these subjects to permit them to produce a high order of results, failure in them justifies the inference of failure in branches whose results are not so directly subject to demonstration. That is to say, we have no right to take it for granted that schools which have proved themselves unable to lead the children to appreciate the relation of numbers, or to express their thoughts in correct and readable English, have for that reason succeeded doubly well in developing their æsthetic and scientific interests, or in leading them to appreciate their relation as individuals to society as a whole.

I therefore maintain that just as the development of character furnishes a highly meritorious supplement to intellectual development in elementary education, but must be in no way accepted as a substitute therefor, so the development of the æsthetic and scientific interests must be looked upon as a valuable addition to thorough instruction in arithmetic and English, and as fully provided for as now in the elementary school curriculum, but must be in no sense accepted as a substitute therefor. And, in consequence, I suggest that, in a comparative study of schools, the three R's shall be regarded as the fundamental standards, and that, while due credit must be given for results in all other branches, no school shall be passed as satisfactory as long as the results in these fail to meet a reasonable demand.

In thus placing the three R's on a pedestal, I do not intend to imply, as I have already indicated, that the schools shall hereafter devote all their time to reading, writing, and arithmetic. On the contrary, I believe that when a clear understanding has been reached as to what ought to be accomplished in these branches, even less time than now will be expended on them. Indeed, the fixing of a minimum result represents but half of the problem before us, the other half being represented by the establishment of maximum limits of time, which my researches have amply proved to lie within our present allotments. Thus, I have shown in previous chapters that excellent results in language and arithmetic may be obtained by devoting forty-five minutes a day to each of those subjects, without any additional study at home, and, furthermore, that if satisfactory results are not obtained within those limits, they are not likely to be obtained at all. And I firmly believe that when our educational work has once been properly systematized, it will be found that the requirements can be fully met if the total appropriation for language, spelling, penmanship, and arithmetic does not exceed two hours a day.

It would be proper, in this connection, to say a word in regard to the relative importance of other subjects, with a view to a wise distribution of credits. But when we look beyond the three R's, questions of creed loom into prominence, and it would carry us too far to enter into a discussion of philosophical problems.

So much then for the theory. Let us now look to its practical application.

What has been stated from the standpoint of theory may be summed up in the following propositions: (1) That the aim of elementary education shall be to develop the higher faculties of the child to the greatest extent to which they can be developed in the elementary schools; (2) that for immediate purposes the range of possibility shall be determined by the best results to be found in our schools to-day; and (3) that all schools shall be held responsible for the maintenance of standards in some measure approaching those maintained in the most successful schools laboring under similar conditions, and that none shall be permitted to fall below a reasonable minimum.

Taking these propositions as a working basis—on the assumption, naturally, that efficiency must be judged by definite achievement—the practical problem becomes resolved into these four questions: (1) Who shall determine what the schools can accomplish and what they may be reasonably expected to accomplish? (2) Who shall decide which schools in a community are, and which of them are not, maintained upon a plane of reasonable expectation? (3) How can the facts be obtained upon which a reasonable minimum may be based? and (4) What can be done to enforce the minimum in every school when it has once been established?

To the first two questions the answer is obvious. The duty of knowing what can and ought to be accomplished in the elementary schools, and of knowing, furthermore, which of the schools are, and which are not, doing satisfactory work, devolves, of course, upon the superintendent; for if supervision has any purpose whatever, it is to see that the schools are conducted upon a plane of reasonable efficiency.

If we accept this much, we must also agree that the fundamental condition of successful supervision is constituted by a knowledge of the best that can be done; for it is evident that the term "efficient service" can convey no definite meaning unless based upon a clear conception of what our most successful teachers have been able to accomplish. And if this be true, it is equally true that the fundamental condition of successful supervision has not yet come into being; for standards in educational achievement are as yet absolutely unknown. In brief, up to the present time, every superintendent has been simply a law unto himself, and supervision has been merely a haphazard affair.

In thus criticising supervision, I desire to emphasize the fact that my remarks are directed against our system of supervision, and not against the superintendents themselves, who, as a rule, are extremely earnest and hard-working people. In a word, the difficulty does not lie with the supervising officers, but is due, fundamentally, to the perverted view that the teacher's efficiency must be estimated by what she knows and by the methods she employs, and not by what she accomplishes. In consequence of this, the supervising officers have largely lost sight of results, and have concentrated their efforts upon observing their teachers at work and upon teaching them psychology and methods. And this in turn has led to the current view that the efficiency of a superintendent must be estimated by the number of visits he pays to the schools, the amount of psychology he knows, the number of teachers' meetings he holds, the breadth of his course of study, the character of his reports, etc., etc., while the actual worth of supervision must not be looked for in the ways and means by which it approaches the educational problem, but in the extent to which it realizes its purposes, *i.e.*, the extent to which the schools succeed in developing intelligence and efficiency in the children; and this can only be tested by testing the intelligence and efficiency of the children.

Proceeding upon the assumption that the degree of success in school achievement can only be estimated in the light of the best that can be done, it is evident that we can have no absolute basis upon which to estimate the degree of efficiency of a teacher or a principal until we shall have succeeded in arriving at a knowledge of the very best that can be done, and at a series of standards based thereon. Of course, taking a common-sense view of the matter, the absolute best must ever remain an ideal conception, ever advancing as we approach it, and ever eluding pursuit. But setting aside all lofty ideals, and remaining well within the province of the practical, it is not only possible, but comparatively easy, to establish a system that will furnish us with the means of relatively distinguishing between strong and weak, good and bad, and of basing upon these: first, a series of ratings which will convey in unmistakable terms the comparative degree of success of every principal and teacher; and, secondly, a minimum demand which could scarcely fail to be approved by reasonable and earnest teachers.

In principle the system is simplicity itself. It consists merely in subjecting the schools from time to time to uniform tests—prepared not from the standpoint of mechanical knowledge, but strictly from that of efficiency—and in recording and tabulating the results. The tests should be taken at the close of the period spent by the children with any one teacher, so that the work of each teacher could be judged by the progress made by her pupils during the entire period that they had spent in her room. But in order that the sins of the teacher may not be visited upon her pupils, the tests must be in no sense regarded as examinations for promotion. Otherwise, few, if any, of the pupils of very weak teachers would ever experience the pleasant sensation of being promoted, as they would be positively unable to make any kind of a showing on tests capable of demonstrating their degree of intelligence and efficiency. However, this danger would be necessarily avoided by the fact that the papers could not be possibly marked and reported upon until long after the promotions had taken place.

At this point a serious objection will be raised on the ground that the spirit of rivalry among the teachers would cause a certain proportion of them—even specialists in moral development—to forget their consciences in their desire to obtain a good rating, so that the class averages might be inversely proportionate to the conscientiousness of the teachers, rather than directly representative of the efficiency of the pupils. But I go farther and say that weakness of conscience is but one of many elements that would have to be considered in taking uniform tests. A source of error of perhaps equal importance is represented by the fact that, even among those whose motives could not be impugned, great irregularities would occur, for the reason that different teachers would observe different standards in marking. Some teachers are so constituted that they cannot help giving pupils the benefit of the doubt, in consequence of which they would be likely to mark the papers very much more leniently than teachers who have no patience with carelessness, and place a premium upon accuracy and precision. Thus, for the reasons mentioned, and many others, it may be stated that while volumes of records based upon uniform tests freely conducted and marked by teachers would be as valuable as any other records of the same dimensions for use in starting a fire, they would be of no value whatever for scientific purposes, and might possibly become a source of corruption.

Whatever is worth doing is worth doing well, and nothing is done well unless placed in charge of some one who can be held responsible for it. And who shall this be? Certainly not the superintendent, who already has more burdens to carry than he is capable of handling with care. The truth is that the necessity of developing definite standards in education has not yet been recognized, and that our school systems are not now prepared to meet the issue. While there is nothing in the plan of testing and recording which is not perfectly practical and feasible, nevertheless its application involves considerable labor of a kind heretofore unknown, and for this provision must be made in the form of a special department of supervision—a department of results, in charge of a supervisor of results.

If asked whether it is worth while to undergo the expense, I must ask whether it pays a railroad or a commercial house to keep any account of its income. The establishment of a department of results would mean neither more nor less than the inauguration of a system of bookkeeping which would enable us to estimate what the children were getting in return for their time and effort, not to descend to the level of inquiring what the people were getting for their money. A perfect system of pedagogical bookkeeping would involve the opening of an account with every teacher and every building, the respective items representing the results achieved in every branch, and not only by a school as a whole, or a class as a whole, but by each individual child as well. Such records as these, if based on tests of efficiency, carefully prepared, carefully given, and followed by a careful marking of the papers, would be reliable records of the efficiency of individual teachers and principals; and the tables prepared from the records, in the order of merit, would show at a glance which of the teachers and schools had been doing efficient work, and which of them had failed to achieve a reasonable minimum. Moreover, such tables would serve to furnish the superintendent with charts enabling him with open eyes to direct his forces where they would do the most good, instead of simply following a routine course in the hope that the seed he sows may here and there take root.

Of course, as I have already indicated, the value of the work would depend entirely on the spirit in which it was done; for if due care should not be exercised, first, in the preparation of the test questions, secondly, in the taking of the tests, and thirdly, in the marking of the papers, the scheme would be worse than useless. Therefore, it would be the duty of the supervisor of results to exercise due care in all these particulars.

1. Of the three points mentioned, the second and third are matters of detail, but the first strikes the keynote of the whole situation; for the nature of the test questions will be representative of the demand, and, as such, will direct the teaching either in the right or the wrong direction. I can see as clearly as any one that under the proposed system lies lurking the old danger of cramming and drilling for examinations; but when a rock has been surmounted by danger signals that can be seen and heard from afar, the ships know enough to keep clear of it, and it ceases to be a menace.

Therefore, if the dangers of the examination system are cramming and mechanical drill, then so prepare your tests that these will be of no avail. In arithmetic, this may be done by giving all questions in the form of problems, which call not only for a knowledge of the fundamental processes, but for independent thought as well. Under these conditions the teachers could not fail to try to get their pupils to acquire not merely a mechanical knowledge of arithmetic, but a thorough grasp of the subject; and that is exactly what we wish them to do. Again, in language we can avoid the dangers of mechanical work by avoiding all technical questions, and limiting them to those calling for the power of expression; and if the teachers should so direct their energies as to lead their pupils to express their thoughts in correct and readable English, then they would here also be doing just what they ought to do, and the danger of the examination in English would also have been turned into a blessing. And if the system should accomplish no more than lead to the development in all schools of a thorough grasp of arithmetic, and the power to produce a creditable piece of work in English, clearly and neatly written, and practically free from mistakes in spelling, then the system would accomplish infinitely more than any other system, as a system, has ever accomplished before, and the teachers would be freer than they have ever been to concentrate, and correlate, and apperceive, and to do all the rest.

I must confess that on the surface the scheme looks very mechanical and sounds very badly; but I take consolation in what some one has said concerning Wagner's music: "It's a great deal better than it sounds." If the questions were formulated from the standpoint of efficiency, the schools could not possibly fall back into the old routine. The fact is that our good schools would be in no way disturbed by the system, which has taken its cue from them; and I confidently believe that nearly all strong teachers and principals would give it their heartiest welcome. What it is intended to do, and cannot fail to do, is simply to start up the circulation of those who will not move without a spur, and to bring those to their senses who do not seem to appreciate the fundamental purpose of the elementary school.

2. As to ways and means of taking the tests so that the papers could be labelled "chemically pure,"

I have no panacea to offer; the matter being one that would have to be decided in accordance with local conditions. That the question should be raised at all is bad enough; but the fact that the teachers themselves recognize the difficulty, and look upon it, more or less, as merely a manifestation of human imperfection, would no doubt cause them to submit with very good grace to any uniform precautions that might be prescribed.

3. While it would be the duty of the supervisor of results to see that due care was exercised in preparing the questions and in conducting the examinations, still these matters would represent mere incidents in his work, while the major portion of his time would be devoted to looking after the results themselves. This would involve care in the marking of the papers—which would have to be sent to his office immediately after collection—and care in recording and in tabulating the results. The detailed labor would, of course, necessitate the employment of assistants, who would have to be trained for this particular kind of work. But the number of clerks required would depend upon how far the community was willing to carry out the project, which could extend from a minimum of marking papers and recording results in the three R's to a maximum which knows no limits. For the purposes of supervision, pure and simple, and limited to spelling, penmanship, language, and arithmetic, my own experience would appear to indicate that assistance at the rate of one clerk for every one hundred and fifty teachers would suffice; and perhaps one clerk to seventy-five

teachers could care for the entire curriculum. But it would be possible to utilize the work of the children for scientific as well as for supervisory purposes, as it would represent material, and the only material, competent to verify pedagogical theories, and the only material out of which a genuine science of pedagogy could ever be constructed. Naturally, however, work upon the papers from a laboratory standpoint would incur additional expense.

But aside from the laboratory idea, the headquarters of the supervisor of results would represent a great deal more than a mere counting-room. In the first place, the work of the children as well as the records being here assembled, the papers would serve the purpose of vouchers whenever the records should be called into question by principals or teachers dissatisfied with their ratings. Up to the present time, the rating of teachers has been a most delicate affair, because superintendents have been obliged in this matter to judge primarily by impressions, in consequence of which it has been next to impossible for them to sustain charges of inefficiency when cross-examined by persons not posted on pedagogical creeds. Under the proposed arrangement, however, all controversies of this nature could be decided, one way or the other, by referring to the work on which the rating was based.

Next, the keeping of the papers in conjunction with the records would serve the purpose of illustrating to teachers what kind of work each rating implied. This object could, perhaps, be most effectively and economically attained through a careful selection of sets of papers representing all shades of differences, from the best to the poorest, in the work of each branch and of every grade. In this manner teachers could learn to appreciate, as they could not in any other way, what can be accomplished and what ought to be accomplished; and then, by comparing the work of their own classes with the selections before them, they could readily judge for themselves at what point in the scale their own results belonged. In the case of class work selected for general inspection, the names of the schools as well as those of the pupils should, for obvious reasons, be removed; but no facts of any kind should be withheld from any of the members of the board of education, and none from the members of the local committee, in matters concerning the schools of their own districts. And teachers who had failed should be entitled to know where the good work had been done, so that they could place themselves in communication with successful teachers, and try to derive as much benefit as possible from them.

That the activities of a department of results would serve, in due course of time, to establish minimum standards is scarcely open to doubt. But the establishment of standards covers only half of the practical side of our problem; the other half being represented by their enforcement when developed. How, then, may the demand be enforced?

Taking the various pros and cons into consideration, it seems to me that, with a definite goal in view, three factors would serve to raise the standard of the weaker schools to a plane of reasonable efficiency.

They are: (1) Self-activity on the part of principals and teachers; (2) local school committees; and (3) tenure of office contingent on efficient service.

By self-activity, I mean improvement resulting from the stimulating effect of the mere existence of a specific and reasonable demand. Among the principals and teachers now employed, there is no doubt that a certain proportion are actually unfit for the positions they occupy. But, on the other hand, it is equally certain that failure under the conditions heretofore existing is by no means, in itself, an indication of incompetence, and that among those who have failed a great many could readily have succeeded if their energies had been properly utilized. In some such instances, perhaps the majority, failure has been due simply to the absence of standards, *i.e.*, to the fact that the principals have had no idea of the capacity of children, and have been laboring under the impression that their pupils were doing very well, when, in truth, they were doing very badly. Next, in a large number of cases, the principals have been led astray either by the belief that results are unimportant or in working out theories that won't work out.

Thus, I am of the opinion that the mere existence of a minimum demand, and of a permanent educational exhibit at headquarters capable of illustrating the nature of that demand, would, in a large number of cases, suffice to bring about the desired result. The first to be affected by the stimulus would no doubt be those who had an unselfish desire to do the best they could for their pupils; the next would be those whose personal pride would cause them to try to keep up with the procession; and, finally, the introduction of the element of competition into school work would touch the chords of ambition, and catch a great many additional ones.

Thus, if the establishment of a minimum demand would serve to set in motion such springs of action as desire, pride, and ambition, we may depend upon it that many of those who have heretofore failed would in the future succeed solely through the influence of self-activity. However, in order that these various motives could be relied upon to play their part, it would be necessary for the principals and teachers to know that what they were doing was being duly appreciated. Therefore, we should be obliged to fortify the demand for good work by introducing into the administration a body of persons whose duty it would be to take an interest and a pride in the schools, and to bring them in close touch with the citizens. Heretofore most of our educational evils have been ascribed to the fact that the people have failed to take an intelligent interest in the schools. However, this apathy has not been the fault of the people, but that of the educators themselves, who have thus far spoken in a language which laymen have been unable to understand, while a department of results would make that language intelligible to them, and serve to bridge over a chasm which until now has been altogether unfathomable.

The existence, at the central office, of records showing the comparative standing of every school in the community could not fail to awaken among intelligent parents a desire to know how the standing of the school attended by their own children compared with that of other schools. To give them an opportunity to gratify this desire, as well as indirectly to exert a moral influence on the schools that are dearest to them, they should be entitled to elect a certain number of representatives clothed with the authority to examine the records, and to whom they could apply for information and advice. I should, therefore, suggest a division of the system into districts containing, say, three buildings each, and the establishment of district committees, composed of three members, elected by the people, those only being eligible who should have resided in the district for a number of years, and who should have children of their own attending the schools.

To what extent the moral influence of the existence of a department of results, fortified by the sympathetic vigilance of the people, would suffice to produce the desired effect, I am, of course, unable to say. But, basing an estimate on my personal knowledge of schools and school people, I have every reason to believe that, within a comparatively brief period, the combination would prove effective in at least fifty per cent of our present failures, and, therefore, that the actual problem would soon become so far reduced that our attention could be concentrated entirely upon probably not over one-third of our total number of schools.

And what could be done with the vexatious third? From a strictly commercial or scientific point of view, or from the standpoint of the rights of the child, the question presents no difficulty whatever, as the cardinal remedy is obviously that of tenure of office contingent upon efficient service. But as the dismissal of principals and teachers is always equivalent to banishing them from the community, and not infrequently to depriving them of the means of earning a living wage, it is evident that, excepting in the case of transients, it should not be applied until all other expedients had failed. In consideration of this fact, the citizens should be granted a certain degree of latitude in the selection of a building, so that no child could be forced to attend a school which was not maintained upon a plane of reasonable efficiency; and, in the absence of the freedom of the entire system, the parents should be permitted to choose at least between any one of the three buildings in their own district. As the question of choice would then naturally serve to place a certain amount of responsibility upon the shoulders of the parents, the central authorities should make it a point to induce especially competent principals to take charge of the schools in those districts where the majority of the parents were not sufficiently enlightened to enable them to make a discriminating selection.

In conclusion, I desire once more to emphasize the fact that the system herein proposed has the advantage of introducing enough definiteness into school-work to afford the plain people an opportunity to take that intelligent interest in the education of their children which has so long seemed desirable. On first consideration, the question of expense cannot fail to militate against its adoption, although this obstacle would not be difficult to overcome, if an increase of two or three per cent in the appropriation for the schools would be made to increase their efficiency by fifty per cent. But ultimately the issue must be decided upon the merits of the plan itself. From my own point of view, the scheme appears attractive not only for the reasons I have stated in this paper, but for any number of additional ones which I have been here unable to mention, and which open up possibilities for the realization of educational ideals far beyond our present conception. For example, in the present chapter I have touched simply upon the development of standards from the side of the schools of individual communities, while the community itself is but an atom in a universal system in which the central position is occupied by the child, whose possibilities recognize no municipal limits. However, as no one is able to form an unprejudiced view of the merits of a scheme of his own invention, I must submit the case to the tender mercies of the reader.

In thus placing the case into the hands of those who are able to form an impartial judgment, I cannot refrain from stating that no one who is sufficiently interested in the plan to give it careful consideration should hesitate to form an opinion on the ground that he is not versed in pedagogical problems; for, whichever side he may choose to espouse, he need not be ashamed of his party. If he should feel inclined to believe that the establishment of a department of results would cause all ideals to fly out of the window and serve to convert the schools into worse machines than they have ever been, he would undoubtedly find himself allied with large numbers of educators whose motives could not be impugned. If, on the other hand, he should prefer to take the side of the writer, he would find himself in the company of numbers of school people of equal rank who feel that the inauguration of such a system as I have described would not be, in any sense, a blow at idealism, but would, on the contrary, afford the schools an opportunity in some measure to realize ideals which until now have been stored away on the shelves of our pedagogical libraries. Consequently, upon the question before us, the position occupied by educators is similar to that of expert witnesses in a case in which it is possible for either side to furnish expert testimony *ad libitum,* but which is ultimately decided by a jury composed of ordinary business men.